ARE YOU

READY
FOR SOME
FOOTBALL?

├──2023──┤

ARE YOU

READY

FOR SOME

FOOTBALL?

Your Pocket Guide to the
2023 National Football League Season

By M. G. Ross

Are You Ready for Some Football?
Your Pocket Guide to the 2023 National Football League Season
By M. G. Ross

Library of Congress Cataloging-In-Publication Data
Ross, M.G.
Are You Ready for Some Football?/ M.G. Ross
ISBN 9798394939075

Cover Design by Amber Colleran

For more information or to contact the author, send emails to
MGRoss.Football@gmail.com

This book is dedicated to my father and grandfather, who inspired in me a love of football, a love of hard work and fair play, and an unapologetic belief in keeping score. Special thanks go to my incomparable designer, Sekayi Brunson, who turned my pen scratchings into what you hold in your hands today, and my cover designer, Amber Colleran, who made sure my crazy idea looks like a real book.

TABLE OF CONTENTS

Introduction

As faithful readers of this series know, when I decided to create an annual football guide, I did it out of frustration. Having loved football since childhood, I listen to sports talk radio religiously, am addicted to the NFL channel, and count the days between Super Bowl Sunday and the start of the pre-season. Like many of you, I watch the combine and the draft (hosted this year by the Super Bowl champions!), and I spend lots of time on ESPN.com and NFL.com, tracking which free agents have signed with new teams, how the draft picks are shaping up, the latest rule changes, and the revolving door of coaches and players.

But there was one thing I needed that I just couldn't find: a convenient, portable, fan-friendly guide to the weekly schedule of games. Sure, you can see the schedule every week online, but I wanted something in print, that I could write on and keep notes on and keep track of, week after week. I could find team schedules for the year, but not a handy full-year schedule that I could print out and use.

So I decided to make one. As I worked on it, I included what I would want, as the prototypical football fan. An easy to read week-by-week schedule. An at-a-glance schedule for each team. Room to keep track of your picks and the final scores. A way to keep track of a team's record throughout the season. A little write-up on each team, including their head coach and their first-round draft pick, plus a reminder of how last season ended and what they've done in the off-season to get ready for this year. And a playoff section, where you can fill in your bracket as the playoffs are about to start, and then track each game throughout the postseason.

That's what you now hold in your hands. I hope you find it useful, and I hope it makes watching football each week even more fun.

As we approach the start of the 2023 season, we seem to have entered the "next generation" of great quarterbacks — and nearly all of them are in the AFC. Meanwhile, some "old" faces are in new places, most notably Aaron Rodgers, sporting a new shade of green in New York. As always, we've got plenty of storylines to track and drama to unfold. But whether your favorite team is a returning champion or due for a rebuild, I'm sure you join me in celebrating the start of another NFL season.

Thanks for your support, and ... hey... it's almost time for kick-off. Gotta go!

M.G.Ross

July 2023

How to Use This Book

As a football fan, you have a pretty good idea of which teams are strong, which teams face a "challenge" and which teams are poised for a break-out. But every season has its share of surprises and disappointments.

This pocket guide is designed to make it fun to watch the games each week, and easy to keep track of your favorite team's record of wins and losses — and the whole league — as the season marches on.

The very first thing I want you to do is to **turn to page 5** and fill out **Your 2023 Season Predictions**. This is your chance to predict, at the very start of the season, who the winners will be when it's all over in January. As a reminder, on **page 4** you'll see all the **NFL Teams by Division and Conference**.

As the regular season starts, the **Weekly Schedules** are your chance to handicap the games in advance, and predict who will win and who will lose each week. I suggest that every Thursday, before the first game of the week starts, you fill out your weekly predictions for that week. Use the **Weekly Schedules** section (starting on page 7) to make your picks, and to keep track of how well you do. At the end of the week (after Monday night's game) tally up your predictions and enter your "score" for the week in the **Scorecard** sheet (page 90). Use this sheet to keep track of your wins and losses each week during the regular season. One note: all game times listed are in Eastern Time.

Most of us have a favorite team (and some of us have a team we love to hate); use the **Team Schedules** (starting on page 25) to keep track of how each team is doing, especially in those all-important divisional match-ups. As the end of the season approaches, you will have a birds-eye view of how the playoffs are shaping up and who is likely to make it to the post-season.

Once the regular season is over, use the **Playoffs** section to make watching the post-season fun. The first thing you'll want to do is to compare those predictions you made at the beginning of the season (back on page 5) with the actual results (fill in your **Division Winners Sheet**, page 93). Then it's time to fill in your bracket: You know who the seven teams are from the NFC and the AFC — enter the teams into the bracket (on your **2023 Playoff Bracket Predictions**, page 96) , and take a shot at predicting who will make it through and wind up in the Super Bowl. Then follow along as the playoffs unfold, using your **2023 Playoff Bracket Tracker** (page 97) to keep track of who advances each week on the road to Super Bowl 58.

NFL Teams By Division and Conference

NFC NORTH

Chicago Bears
Detroit Lions
Green Bay Packers
Minnesota Vikings

NFC SOUTH

Atlanta Falcons
Carolina Panthers
New Orleans Saints
Tampa Bay Buccaneers

NFC EAST

Dallas Cowboys
New York Giants
Philadelphia Eagles
Washington Commanders

NFC WEST

Arizona Cardinals
Los Angeles Rams
San Francisco 49ers
Seattle Seahawks

AFC NORTH

Baltimore Ravens
Cincinnati Bengals
Cleveland Browns
Pittsburgh Steelers

AFC SOUTH

Houston Texans
Indianapolis Colts
Jacksonville Jaguars
Tennessee Titans

AFC EAST

Buffalo Bills
Miami Dolphins
New England Patriots
New York Jets

AFC WEST

Denver Broncos
Kansas City Chiefs
Las Vegas Raiders
Los Angeles Chargers

Your 2023 Season Predictions

Fill this in before the season even starts — can you predict who's going to win each division — and who the wildcard teams will be?

AFC

Division Winners:

North	_____
South	_____
East	_____
West	_____

Wild Card 1 _____

Wild Card 2 _____

Wild Card 3 _____

NFC

Division Winners:

North	_____
South	_____
East	_____
West	_____

Wild Card 1 _____

Wild Card 2 _____

Wild Card 3 _____

WEEKLY SCHEDULES

WEEK 1: September 7-11

Pick your winners before the games start, then keep track of the scores as they happen

Thursday Night Game

☐ Detroit Lions   ☐ at Kansas City Chiefs   8:20 pm   ___
Final Score: _____ v. _____

Sunday Games

☐ Arizona Cardinals   ☐ at Washington Commanders 1 pm   ___
Final Score: _____ v. _____

☐ Carolina Panthers   ☐ at Atlanta Falcons   ___
Final Score: _____ v. _____

☐ Cincinnati Bengals   ☐ at Cleveland Browns   ___
Final Score: _____ v. _____

☐ Houston Texans   ☐ at Baltimore Ravens   ___
Final Score: _____ v. _____

☐ Jacksonville Jaguars   ☐ at Indianapolis Colts   ___
Final Score: _____ v. _____

☐ San Francisco 49ers   ☐ at Pittsburgh Steelers   ___
Final Score: _____ v. _____

☐ Tampa Bay Buccaneers   ☐ at Minnesota Vikings   ___
Final Score: _____ v. _____

☐ Tennessee Titans   ☐ at New Orleans Saints   ___
Final Score: _____ v. _____

☐ Green Bay Packers   ☐ at Chicago Bears   4 pm   ___
Final Score: _____ v. _____

☐ Las Vegas Raiders   ☐ at Denver Broncos   ___
Final Score: _____ v. _____

☐ Los Angeles Rams   ☐ at Seattle Seahawks   ___
Final Score: _____ v. _____

☐ Miami Dolphins   ☐ at Los Angeles Chargers   ___
Final Score: _____ v. _____

☐ Philadelphia Eagles   ☐ at New England Patriots   ___
Final Score: _____ v. _____

Sunday Night Game

☐ Dallas Cowboys   ☐ at New York Giants   8:20 pm   ___
Final Score: _____ v. _____

Monday Night Game

☐ Buffalo Bills   ☐ at New York Jets   8:15 pm   ___
Final Score: _____ v. _____

WEEK 2: September 14-18

ick your winners before the games start, then keep track of the scores as they happen.

hursday Night Game

☐ Minnesota Vikings ☐ at Philadelphia Eagles 8:15 pm ____
Final Score: _____ v. _____

unday Games

☐ Baltimore Ravens ☐ at Cincinnati Bengals 1 pm ____
Final Score: _____ v. _____

☐ Chicago Bears ☐ at Tampa Bay Buccaneers ____
Final Score: _____ v. _____

☐ Green Bay Packers ☐ at Atlanta Falcons ____
Final Score: _____ v. _____

☐ Indianapolis Colts ☐ at Houston Texans ____
Final Score: _____ v. _____

☐ Kansas City Chiefs ☐ at Jacksonville Jaguars ____
Final Score: _____ v. _____

☐ Las Vegas Raiders ☐ at Buffalo Bills ____
Final Score: _____ v. _____

☐ Los Angeles Chargers ☐ at Tennessee Titans ____
Final Score: _____ v. _____

☐ Seattle Seahawks ☐ at Detroit Lions ____
Final Score: _____ v. _____

☐ New York Giants ☐ at Arizona Cardinals 4 pm ____
Final Score: _____ v. _____

☐ New York Jets ☐ at Dallas Cowboys ____
Final Score: _____ v. _____

☐ San Francisco 49ers ☐ at Los Angeles Rams ____
Final Score: _____ v. _____

☐ Washington Commanders ☐ at Denver Broncos ____
Final Score: _____ v. _____

unday Night Game

☐ Miami Dolphins ☐ at New England Patriots 8:20 pm ____
Final Score: _____ v. _____

onday Night Games

☐ New Orleans Saints ☐ at Carolina Panthers 7:15 pm ____
Final Score: _____ v. _____

☐ Cleveland Browns ☐ at Pittsburgh Steelers 8:30 pm ____
Final Score: _____ v. _____

WEEK 3: September 21-25

Pick your winners before the games start, then keep track of the scores as they happe.

Thursday Night Game

☐ New York Giants ☐ at San Francisco 49ers 8:15 pm ___
Final Score: _____ v. _____

Sunday Games

☐ Atlanta Falcons ☐ at Detroit Lions 1 pm ___
Final Score: _____ v. _____

☐ Buffalo Bills ☐ at Washington Commanders ___
Final Score: _____ v. _____

☐ Denver Broncos ☐ at Miami Dolphins ___
Final Score: _____ v. _____

☐ Houston Texans ☐ at Jacksonville Jaguars ___
Final Score: _____ v. _____

☐ Indianapolis Colts ☐ at Baltimore Ravens ___
Final Score: _____ v. _____

☐ Los Angeles Chargers ☐ at Minnesota Vikings ___
Final Score: _____ v. _____

☐ New England Patriots ☐ at New York Jets ___
Final Score: _____ v. _____

☐ New Orleans Saints ☐ at Green Bay Packers ___
Final Score: _____ v. _____

☐ Tennessee Titans ☐ at Cleveland Browns ___
Final Score: _____ v. _____

☐ Carolina Panthers ☐ at Seattle Seahawks 4 pm ___
Final Score: _____ v. _____

☐ Chicago Bears ☐ at Kansas City Chiefs ___
Final Score: _____ v. _____

☐ Dallas Cowboys ☐ at Arizona Cardinals ___
Final Score: _____ v. _____

Sunday Night Game

☐ Pittsburgh Steelers ☐ at Las Vegas Raiders 8:20 pm ___
Final Score: _____ v. _____

Monday Night Games

☐ Philadelphia Eagles ☐ at Tampa Bay Buccaneers 7:15 pm ___
Final Score: _____ v. _____

☐ Los Angeles Rams ☐ at Cincinnati Bengals 8:15 pm ___
Final Score: _____ v. _____

WEEK 4: September 28-October 2

Pick your winners before the games start, then keep track of the scores as they happen.

Thursday Night Game

☐ Detroit Lions   ☐ at Green Bay Packers   8:15 pm   ___
      Final Score: _____ v. _____

Sunday Games

☐ Atlanta Falcons   ☐ at Jacksonville Jaguars   9:30 am   ___
      Final Score: _____ v. _____

☐ Baltimore Ravens   ☐ at Cleveland Browns   1 pm   ___
      Final Score: _____ v. _____

☐ Cincinnati Bengals   ☐ at Tennessee Titans   ___
      Final Score: _____ v. _____

☐ Denver Broncos   ☐ at Chicago Bears   ___
      Final Score: _____ v. _____

☐ Los Angeles Rams   ☐ at Indianapolis Colts   ___
      Final Score: _____ v. _____

☐ Miami Dolphins   ☐ at Buffalo Bills   ___
      Final Score: _____ v. _____

☐ Minnesota Vikings   ☐ at Carolina Panthers   ___
      Final Score: _____ v. _____

☐ Pittsburgh Steelers   ☐ at Houston Texans   ___
      Final Score: _____ v. _____

☐ Tampa Bay Buccaneers   ☐ at New Orleans Saints   ___
      Final Score: _____ v. _____

☐ Washington Commanders   ☐ at Philadelphia Eagles   ___
      Final Score: _____ v. _____

☐ Arizona Cardinals   ☐ at San Francisco 49ers   4 pm   ___
      Final Score: _____ v. _____

☐ Las Vegas Raiders   ☐ at Los Angeles Chargers   ___
      Final Score: _____ v. _____

☐ New England Patriots   ☐ at Dallas Cowboys   ___
      Final Score: _____ v. _____

Sunday Night Game

☐ Kansas City Chiefs   ☐ at New York Jets   8:20 pm   ___
      Final Score: _____ v. _____

Monday Night Game

☐ Seattle Seahawks   ☐ at New York Giants   8:15 pm   ___
      Final Score: _____ v. _____

WEEK 5: October 5-9

Pick your winners before the games start, then keep track of the scores as they happen

			✓ Your Correct Pick
Thursday Night Game			
☐ Chicago Bears	☐ at Washington Commanders	8:15 pm	___
Final Score: _____ v. _____			
Sunday Games			
☐ Jacksonville Jaguars	☐ at Buffalo Bills	9:30 am	___
Final Score: _____ v. _____			
☐ Baltimore Ravens	☐ at Pittsburgh Steelers	1 pm	___
Final Score: _____ v. _____			
☐ Carolina Panthers	☐ at Detroit Lions		___
Final Score: _____ v. _____			
☐ Houston Texans	☐ at Atlanta Falcons		___
Final Score: _____ v. _____			
☐ New Orleans Saints	☐ at New England Patriots		___
Final Score: _____ v. _____			
☐ New York Giants	☐ at Miami Dolphins		___
Final Score: _____ v. _____			
☐ Tennessee Titans	☐ at Indianapolis Colts		___
Final Score: _____ v. _____			
☐ Cincinnati Bengals	☐ at Arizona Cardinals	4 pm	___
Final Score: _____ v. _____			
☐ Kansas City Chiefs	☐ at Minnesota Vikings		___
Final Score: _____ v. _____			
☐ New York Jets	☐ at Denver Broncos		___
Final Score: _____ v. _____			
☐ Philadelphia Eagles	☐ at Los Angeles Rams		___
Final Score: _____ v. _____			
Sunday Night Game			
☐ Dallas Cowboys	☐ at San Francisco 49ers	8:20 pm	___
Final Score: _____ v. _____			
Monday Night Game			
☐ Green Bay Packers	☐ at Las Vegas Raiders	8:15 pm	___
Final Score: _____ v. _____			

Teams with a bye: *Cleveland Browns, Los Angeles Chargers, Seattle Seahawks, Tampa Bay Buccaneers*

WEEK 6: October 12-16

Pick your winners before the games start, then keep track of the scores as they happen.

Thursday Night Game

☐ Denver Broncos   ☐ at Kansas City Chiefs   8:15 pm   ___
Final Score: _____ v. _____

Sunday Games

☐ Baltimore Ravens   ☐ at Tennessee Titans   9:30 am   ___
Final Score: _____ v. _____

☐ Carolina Panthers   ☐ at Miami Dolphins   1 pm   ___
Final Score: _____ v. _____

☐ Detroit Lions   ☐ at Tampa Bay Buccaneers   ___
Final Score: _____ v. _____

☐ Indianapolis Colts   ☐ at Jacksonville Jaguars   ___
Final Score: _____ v. _____

☐ Minnesota Vikings   ☐ at Chicago Bears   ___
Final Score: _____ v. _____

☐ New Orleans Saints   ☐ at Houston Texans   ___
Final Score: _____ v. _____

☐ San Francisco 49ers   ☐ at Cleveland Browns   ___
Final Score: _____ v. _____

☐ Seattle Seahawks   ☐ at Cincinnati Bengals   ___
Final Score: _____ v. _____

☐ Washington Commanders ☐ at Atlanta Falcons   ___
Final Score: _____ v. _____

☐ Arizona Cardinals   ☐ at Los Angeles Rams   4 pm   ___
Final Score: _____ v. _____

☐ New England Patriots   ☐ at Las Vegas Raiders   ___
Final Score: _____ v. _____

☐ Philadelphia Eagles   ☐ at New York Jets   ___
Final Score: _____ v. _____

Sunday Night Game

☐ New York Giants   ☐ at Buffalo Bills   8:20 pm   ___
Final Score: _____ v. _____

Monday Night Game

☐ Dallas Cowboys   ☐ at Los Angeles Chargers   8:15 pm   ___
Final Score: _____ v. _____

Teams with a bye: *Green Bay Packers, Pittsburgh Steelers*

WEEK 7: October 19-23

Pick your winners before the games start, then keep track of the scores as they happen

Thursday Night Game

☐ Jacksonville Jaguars   ☐ at New Orleans Saints   8:15 pm   ___
Final Score: _____ v. _____

Sunday Games

☐ Atlanta Falcons   ☐ at Tampa Bay Buccaneers   1 pm   ___
Final Score: _____ v. _____

☐ Buffalo Bills   ☐ at New England Patriots   ___
Final Score: _____ v. _____

☐ Cleveland Browns   ☐ at Indianapolis Colts   ___
Final Score: _____ v. _____

☐ Detroit Lions   ☐ at Baltimore Ravens   ___
Final Score: _____ v. _____

☐ Las Vegas Raiders   ☐ at Chicago Bears   ___
Final Score: _____ v. _____

☐ Washington Commanders   ☐ at New York Giants   ___
Final Score: _____ v. _____

☐ Arizona Cardinals   ☐ at Seattle Seahawks   4 pm   ___
Final Score: _____ v. _____

☐ Green Bay Packers   ☐ at Denver Broncos   ___
Final Score: _____ v. _____

☐ Los Angeles Chargers   ☐ at Kansas City Chiefs   ___
Final Score: _____ v. _____

☐ Pittsburgh Steelers   ☐ at Los Angeles Rams   ___
Final Score: _____ v. _____

Sunday Night Game

☐ Miami Dolphins   ☐ at Philadelphia Eagles   8:20 pm   ___
Final Score: _____ v. _____

Monday Night Game

☐ San Francisco 49ers   ☐ at Minnesota Vikings   8:15 pm   ___
Final Score: _____ v. _____

*Teams with a bye: Carolina Panthers, Cincinnati Bengals, Dallas Cowboys,
Houston Texans, New York Jets, Tennessee Titans*

WEEK 8: October 26-30

Pick your winners before the games start, then keep track of the scores as they happen.

Thursday Night Game

☐ Tampa Bay Buccaneers ☐ at Buffalo Bills 8:15 pm ___
Final Score: _____ v. _____

Sunday Games

☐ Atlanta Falcons ☐ at Tennessee Titans 1 pm ___
Final Score: _____ v. _____

☐ Houston Texans ☐ at Carolina Panthers ___
Final Score: _____ v. _____

☐ Jacksonville Jaguars ☐ at Pittsburgh Steelers ___
Final Score: _____ v. _____

☐ Los Angeles Rams ☐ at Dallas Cowboys ___
Final Score: _____ v. _____

☐ Minnesota Vikings ☐ at Green Bay Packers ___
Final Score: _____ v. _____

☐ New England Patriots ☐ at Miami Dolphins ___
Final Score: _____ v. _____

☐ New Orleans Saints ☐ at Indianapolis Colts ___
Final Score: _____ v. _____

☐ New York Jets ☐ at New York Giants ___
Final Score: _____ v. _____

☐ Philadelphia Eagles ☐ at Washington Commanders ___
Final Score: _____ v. _____

☐ Baltimore Ravens ☐ at Arizona Cardinals 4 pm ___
Final Score: _____ v. _____

☐ Cincinnati Bengals ☐ at San Francisco 49ers ___
Final Score: _____ v. _____

☐ Cleveland Browns ☐ at Seattle Seahawks ___
Final Score: _____ v. _____

☐ Kansas City Chiefs ☐ at Denver Broncos ___
Final Score: _____ v. _____

Sunday Night Game

☐ Chicago Bears ☐ at Los Angeles Chargers 8:20 pm ___
Final Score: _____ v. _____

Monday Night Game

☐ Las Vegas Raiders ☐ at Detroit Lions 8:15 pm ___
Final Score: _____ v. _____

WEEK 9: November 2-6

Pick your winners before the games start, then keep track of the scores as they happen

| | | ✓ Your Correct Pick |

Thursday Night Game

☐ Tennessee Titans ☐ at Pittsburgh Steelers 8:15 pm ___
Final Score: _____ v. _____

Sunday Games

☐ Miami Dolphins ☐ at Kansas City Chiefs 9:30 am ___
Final Score: _____ v. _____

☐ Arizona Cardinals ☐ at Cleveland Browns 1 pm ___
Final Score: _____ v. _____

☐ Chicago Bears ☐ at New Orleans Saints ___
Final Score: _____ v. _____

☐ Los Angeles Rams ☐ at Green Bay Packers ___
Final Score: _____ v. _____

☐ Minnesota Vikings ☐ at Atlanta Falcons ___
Final Score: _____ v. _____

☐ Seattle Seahawks ☐ at Baltimore Ravens ___
Final Score: _____ v. _____

☐ Tampa Bay Buccaneers ☐ at Houston Texans ___
Final Score: _____ v. _____

☐ Washington Commanders ☐ at New England Patriots ___
Final Score: _____ v. _____

☐ Dallas Cowboys ☐ at Philadelphia Eagles 4 pm ___
Final Score: _____ v. _____

☐ Indianapolis Colts ☐ at Carolina Panthers ___
Final Score: _____ v. _____

☐ New York Giants ☐ at Las Vegas Raiders ___
Final Score: _____ v. _____

Sunday Night Game

☐ Buffalo Bills ☐ at Cincinnati Bengals 8:20 pm ___
Final Score: _____ v. _____

Monday Night Game

☐ Los Angeles Chargers ☐ at New York Jets 8:15 pm ___
Final Score: _____ v. _____

Teams with a bye: *Denver Broncos, Detroit Lions, Jacksonville Jaguars, San Francisco 49ers*

WEEK 10: November 9-13

ck your winners before the games start, then keep track of the scores as they happen.

ursday Night Game

☐ Carolina Panthers ☐ at Chicago Bears 8:15 pm ___
Final Score: ___ v. ___

nday Games

☐ Indianapolis Colts ☐ at New England Patriots 9:30 am ___
Final Score: ___ v. ___

☐ Cleveland Browns ☐ at Baltimore Ravens 1 pm ___
Final Score: ___ v. ___

☐ Green Bay Packers ☐ at Pittsburgh Steelers ___
Final Score: ___ v. ___

☐ Houston Texans ☐ at Cincinnati Bengals ___
Final Score: ___ v. ___

☐ New Orleans Saints ☐ at Minnesota Vikings ___
Final Score: ___ v. ___

☐ San Francisco 49ers ☐ at Jacksonville Jaguars ___
Final Score: ___ v. ___

☐ Tennessee Titans ☐ at Tampa Bay Buccaneers ___
Final Score: ___ v. ___

☐ Atlanta Falcons ☐ at Arizona Cardinals 4 pm ___
Final Score: ___ v. ___

☐ Detroit Lions ☐ at Los Angeles Chargers ___
Final Score: ___ v. ___

☐ New York Giants ☐ at Dallas Cowboys ___
Final Score: ___ v. ___

☐ Washington Commanders ☐ at Seattle Seahawks ___
Final Score: ___ v. ___

nday Night Game

☐ New York Jets ☐ at Las Vegas Raiders 8:20 pm ___
Final Score: ___ v. ___

onday Night Game

☐ Denver Broncos ☐ at Buffalo Bills 8:15 pm ___
Final Score: ___ v. ___

ams with a bye: Kansas City Chiefs, Los Angeles Rams, Miami Dolphins,
Philadelphia Eagles

WEEK 11: November 16-20

Pick your winners before the games start, then keep track of the scores as they happe

Thursday Night Game

☐ Cincinnati Bengals   ☐ at Baltimore Ravens   8:15 pm   ___
Final Score: _____ v. _____

Sunday Games

☐ Arizona Cardinals   ☐ at Houston Texans   1 pm   ___
Final Score: _____ v. _____

☐ Chicago Bears   ☐ at Detroit Lions   ___
Final Score: _____ v. _____

☐ Dallas Cowboys   ☐ at Carolina Panthers   ___
Final Score: _____ v. _____

☐ Las Vegas Raiders   ☐ at Miami Dolphins   ___
Final Score: _____ v. _____

☐ Los Angeles Chargers   ☐ at Green Bay Packers   ___
Final Score: _____ v. _____

☐ New York Giants   ☐ at Washington Commanders   ___
Final Score: _____ v. _____

☐ Pittsburgh Steelers   ☐ at Cleveland Browns   ___
Final Score: _____ v. _____

☐ Tennessee Titans   ☐ at Jacksonville Jaguars   ___
Final Score: _____ v. _____

☐ New York Jets   ☐ at Buffalo Bills   4 pm   ___
Final Score: _____ v. _____

☐ Seattle Seahawks   ☐ at Los Angeles Rams   ___
Final Score: _____ v. _____

☐ Tampa Bay Buccaneers   ☐ at San Francisco 49ers   ___
Final Score: _____ v. _____

Sunday Night Game

☐ Minnesota Vikings   ☐ at Denver Broncos   8:20 pm   ___
Final Score: _____ v. _____

Monday Night Game

☐ Philadelphia Eagles   ☐ at Kansas City Chiefs   8:15 pm   ___
Final Score: _____ v. _____

Teams with a bye: *Atlanta Falcons, Indianapolis Colts, New England Patriots,*
New Orleans Saints

WEEK 12: November 23-27

Pick your winners before the games start, then keep track of the scores as they happen.

Thanksgiving Day Games			✓ Your Correct Picks
☐ Green Bay Packers	☐ at Detroit Lions	12:30 pm	___
Final Score: _____ v. _____			
☐ Washington Commanders	☐ at Dallas Cowboys	4:30 pm	___
Final Score: _____ v. _____			
☐ San Francisco 49ers	☐ at Seattle Seahawks	8:20 pm	___
Final Score: _____ v. _____			

Black Friday Game

☐ Miami Dolphins	☐ at New York Jets	3 pm	___
Final Score: _____ v. _____			

Sunday Games

☐ Carolina Panthers	☐ at Tennessee Titans	1 pm	___
Final Score: _____ v. _____			
☐ Jacksonville Jaguars	☐ at Houston Texans		___
Final Score: _____ v. _____			
☐ New England Patriots	☐ at New York Giants		___
Final Score: _____ v. _____			
☐ New Orleans Saints	☐ at Atlanta Falcons		___
Final Score: _____ v. _____			
☐ Pittsburgh Steelers	☐ at Cincinnati Bengals		___
Final Score: _____ v. _____			
☐ Tampa Bay Buccaneers	☐ at Indianapolis Colts		___
Final Score: _____ v. _____			
☐ Buffalo Bills	☐ at Philadelphia Eagles	4 pm	___
Final Score: _____ v. _____			
☐ Cleveland Browns	☐ at Denver Broncos		___
Final Score: _____ v. _____			
☐ Kansas City Chiefs	☐ at Las Vegas Raiders		___
Final Score: _____ v. _____			
☐ Los Angeles Rams	☐ at Arizona Cardinals		___
Final Score: _____ v. _____			

Sunday Night Game

☐ Baltimore Ravens	☐ at Los Angeles Chargers	8:20 pm	___
Final Score: _____ v. _____			

Monday Night Game

☐ Chicago Bears	☐ at Minnesota Vikings	8:15 pm	___
Final Score: _____ v. _____			

WEEK 13: November 30-December 4

Pick your winners before the games start, then keep track of the scores as they happen

Thursday Night Game

☐ Seattle Seahawks ☐ at Dallas Cowboys 8:15 pm ___

Final Score: _____ v. _____

Sunday Games

☐ Arizona Cardinals ☐ at Pittsburgh Steelers 1 pm ___

Final Score: _____ v. _____

☐ Atlanta Falcons ☐ at New York Jets ___

Final Score: _____ v. _____

☐ Carolina Panthers ☐ at Tampa Bay Buccaneers ___

Final Score: _____ v. _____

☐ Detroit Lions ☐ at New Orleans Saints ___

Final Score: _____ v. _____

☐ Indianapolis Colts ☐ at Tennessee Titans ___

Final Score: _____ v. _____

☐ Los Angeles Chargers ☐ at New England Patriots ___

Final Score: _____ v. _____

☐ Miami Dolphins ☐ at Washington Commanders ___

Final Score: _____ v. _____

☐ Cleveland Browns ☐ at Los Angeles Rams 4 pm ___

Final Score: _____ v. _____

☐ Denver Broncos ☐ at Houston Texans ___

Final Score: _____ v. _____

☐ San Francisco 49ers ☐ at Philadelphia Eagles ___

Final Score: _____ v. _____

Sunday Night Game

☐ Kansas City Chiefs ☐ at Green Bay Packers 8:20 pm ___

Final Score: _____ v. _____

Monday Night Game

☐ Cincinnati Bengals ☐ at Jacksonville Jaguars 8:15 pm ___

Final Score: _____ v. _____

Teams with a bye: *Baltimore Ravens, Buffalo Bills, Chicago Bears, Las Vegas Raiders, Minnesota Vikings, New York Giants*

WEEK 14: December 7-11

ck your winners before the games start, then keep track of the scores as they happen.

			✓ Your Correct Picks

ursday Night Game

☐ New England Patriots   ☐ at Pittsburgh Steelers   8:15 pm   ___
     Final Score: _____ v. _____

nday Games

☐ Carolina Panthers   ☐ at New Orleans Saints   1 pm   ___
     Final Score: _____ v. _____

☐ Detroit Lions   ☐ at Chicago Bears   ___
     Final Score: _____ v. _____

☐ Houston Texans   ☐ at New York Jets   ___
     Final Score: _____ v. _____

☐ Indianapolis Colts   ☐ at Cincinnati Bengals   ___
     Final Score: _____ v. _____

☐ Jacksonville Jaguars   ☐ at Cleveland Browns   ___
     Final Score: _____ v. _____

☐ Los Angeles Rams   ☐ at Baltimore Ravens   ___
     Final Score: _____ v. _____

☐ Tampa Bay Buccaneers   ☐ at Atlanta Falcons   ___
     Final Score: _____ v. _____

☐ Buffalo Bills   ☐ at Kansas City Chiefs   4 pm   ___
     Final Score: _____ v. _____

☐ Denver Broncos   ☐ at Los Angeles Chargers   ___
     Final Score: _____ v. _____

☐ Minnesota Vikings   ☐ at Las Vegas Raiders   ___
     Final Score: _____ v. _____

☐ Seattle Seahawks   ☐ at San Francisco 49ers   ___
     Final Score: _____ v. _____

nday Night Game

☐ Philadelphia Eagles   ☐ at Dallas Cowboys   8:20 pm   ___
     Final Score: _____ v. _____

onday Night Games

☐ Green Bay Packers   ☐ at New York Giants   8:15 pm   ___
     Final Score: _____ v. _____

☐ Tennessee Titans   ☐ at Miami Dolphins   ___
     Final Score: _____ v. _____

ams with a bye: *Arizona Cardinals, Washington Commanders*

Pick your winners before the games start, then keep track of the scores as they happen

			✓ Your Correct Pick
Thursday Night Game			
☐ Los Angeles Chargers	☐ at Las Vegas Raiders	8:15 pm	___
Final Score: _____ v. _____			
Sunday Games			
☐ Atlanta Falcons	☐ at Carolina Panthers	TBD	___
Final Score: _____ v. _____			
☐ Chicago Bears	☐ at Cleveland Browns		___
Final Score: _____ v. _____			
☐ Denver Broncos	☐ at Detroit Lions		___
Final Score: _____ v. _____			
☐ Minnesota Vikings	☐ at Cincinnati Bengals		___
Final Score: _____ v. _____			
☐ Pittsburgh Steelers	☐ at Indianapolis Colts		___
Final Score: _____ v. _____			
☐ Houston Texans	☐ at Tennessee Titans	1 pm	___
Final Score: _____ v. _____			
☐ New York Giants	☐ at New Orleans Saints		___
Final Score: _____ v. _____			
☐ New York Jets	☐ at Miami Dolphins		___
Final Score: _____ v. _____			
☐ Tampa Bay Buccaneers	☐ at Green Bay Packers		___
Final Score: _____ v. _____			
☐ Dallas Cowboys	☐ at Buffalo Bills	4 pm	___
Final Score: _____ v. _____			
☐ Philadelphia Eagles	☐ at Seattle Seahawks		___
Final Score: _____ v. _____			
☐ San Francisco 49ers	☐ at Arizona Cardinals		___
Final Score: _____ v. _____			
☐ Washington Commanders	☐ at Los Angeles Rams		___
Final Score: _____ v. _____			
Sunday Night Game			
☐ Baltimore Ravens	☐ at Jacksonville Jaguars	8:20 pm	___
Final Score: _____ v. _____			
Monday Night Game			
☐ Kansas City Chiefs	☐ at New England Patriots	8:15 pm	___
Final Score: _____ v. _____			

WEEK 16: December 21-25

ick your winners before the games start, then keep track of the scores as they happen.

			✓ Your Correct Picks
hursday Night Game			
☐ New Orleans Saints	☐ at Los Angeles Rams	8:15 pm	___
Final Score: _____ v. _____			
aturday Games			
☐ Cincinnati Bengals	☐ at Pittsburgh Steelers	4:30 pm	___
Final Score: _____ v. _____			
☐ Buffalo Bills	☐ at Los Angeles Chargers	8 pm	___
Final Score: _____ v. _____			
unday Games			
☐ Cleveland Browns	☐ at Houston Texans	1 pm	___
Final Score: _____ v. _____			
☐ Detroit Lions	☐ at Minnesota Vikings		___
Final Score: _____ v. _____			
☐ Green Bay Packers	☐ at Carolina Panthers		___
Final Score: _____ v. _____			
☐ Indianapolis Colts	☐ at Atlanta Falcons		___
Final Score: _____ v. _____			
☐ Seattle Seahawks	☐ at Tennessee Titans		___
Final Score: _____ v. _____			
☐ Washington Commanders	☐ at New York Jets		___
Final Score: _____ v. _____			
☐ Arizona Cardinals	☐ at Chicago Bears	4 pm	___
Final Score: _____ v. _____			
☐ Dallas Cowboys	☐ at Miami Dolphins		___
Final Score: _____ v. _____			
☐ Jacksonville Jaguars	☐ at Tampa Bay Buccaneers		___
Final Score: _____ v. _____			
unday Night Game			
☐ New England Patriots	☐ at Denver Broncos	8:15 pm	___
Final Score: _____ v. _____			
hristmas Day Games			
☐ Las Vegas Raiders	☐ at Kansas City Chiefs	1 pm	___
Final Score: _____ v. _____			
☐ New York Giants	☐ at Philadelphia Eagles	4:30 pm	___
Final Score: _____ v. _____			
☐ Baltimore Ravens	☐ at San Francisco 49ers	8:15 pm	___
Final Score: _____ v. _____			

WEEK 17: December 28-31

Pick your winners before the games start, then keep track of the scores as they happen

Thursday Night Game

☐ New York Jets   ☐ at Cleveland Browns   8:15 pm   ___
Final Score: _____ v. _____

Saturday Night Game

☐ Detroit Lions   ☐ at Dallas Cowboys   8:15 pm   ___
Final Score: _____ v. _____

Sunday Games

☐ Arizona Cardinals   ☐ at Philadelphia Eagles   1 pm   ___
Final Score: _____ v. _____

☐ Atlanta Falcons   ☐ at Chicago Bears   ___
Final Score: _____ v. _____

☐ Carolina Panthers   ☐ at Jacksonville Jaguars   ___
Final Score: _____ v. _____

☐ Las Vegas Raiders   ☐ at Indianapolis Colts   ___
Final Score: _____ v. _____

☐ Los Angeles Rams   ☐ at New York Giants   ___
Final Score: _____ v. _____

☐ Miami Dolphins   ☐ at Baltimore Ravens   ___
Final Score: _____ v. _____

☐ New England Patriots   ☐ at Buffalo Bills   ___
Final Score: _____ v. _____

☐ New Orleans Saints   ☐ at Tampa Bay Buccaneers   ___
Final Score: _____ v. _____

☐ San Francisco 49ers   ☐ at Washington Commanders   ___
Final Score: _____ v. _____

☐ Tennessee Titans   ☐ at Houston Texans   ___
Final Score: _____ v. _____

☐ Cincinnati Bengals   ☐ at Kansas City Chiefs   4 pm   ___
Final Score: _____ v. _____

☐ Los Angeles Chargers   ☐ at Denver Broncos   ___
Final Score: _____ v. _____

☐ Pittsburgh Steelers   ☐ at Seattle Seahawks   ___
Final Score: _____ v. _____

Sunday Night Game

☐ Green Bay Packers   ☐ at Minnesota Vikings   8:20 pm   ___
Final Score: _____ v. _____

WEEK 18: January 7

Pick your winners before the games start, then keep track of the scores as they happen.

Sunday Games (All Times TBD)		✓ Your Correct Picks
☐ Atlanta Falcons	☐ at New Orleans Saints	___
Final Score: _____ v. _____		
☐ Buffalo Bills	☐ at Miami Dolphins	___
Final Score: _____ v. _____		
☐ Chicago Bears	☐ at Green Bay Packers	___
Final Score: _____ v. _____		
☐ Cleveland Browns	☐ at Cincinnati Bengals	___
Final Score: _____ v. _____		
☐ Dallas Cowboys	☐ at Washington Commanders	___
Final Score: _____ v. _____		
☐ Denver Broncos	☐ at Las Vegas Raiders	___
Final Score: _____ v. _____		
☐ Houston Texans	☐ at Indianapolis Colts	___
Final Score: _____ v. _____		
☐ Jacksonville Jaguars	☐ at Tennessee Titans	___
Final Score: _____ v. _____		
☐ Kansas City Chiefs	☐ at Los Angeles Chargers	___
Final Score: _____ v. _____		
☐ Los Angeles Rams	☐ at San Francisco 49ers	___
Final Score: _____ v. _____		
☐ Minnesota Vikings	☐ at Detroit Lions	___
Final Score: _____ v. _____		
☐ New York Jets	☐ at New England Patriots	___
Final Score: _____ v. _____		
☐ Philadelphia Eagles	☐ at New York Giants	___
Final Score: _____ v. _____		
☐ Pittsburgh Steelers	☐ at Baltimore Ravens	___
Final Score: _____ v. _____		
☐ Seattle Seahawks	☐ at Arizona Cardinals	___
Final Score: _____ v. _____		
☐ Tampa Bay Buccaneers	☐ at Carolina Panthers	___
Final Score: _____ v. _____		

TEAM SCHEDULES

ARIZONA CARDINALS

Head Coach: Jonathan Gannon* | 2022 Record: 4-13

First Round Draft Pick: Paris Johnson Jr., OT (6)

new head coa

Going in the wrong direction. That's the feeling we got throughout the 2022 season, even before Kyler Murray tore his ACL in week 14 and Arizona limped through the last few games with Colt McCoy under center. The scene off the field might have been worse, with the GM taking a health-related leave of absence and an assistant coach fired for sexual assault, and then suing the team. As the 2023 season draws near, both the head coach and the GM are out — and it's unclear how long Murray himself will be out as he recovers from his late-season injury. Losing their single most talented player, DeAndre Hopkins, won't help matters either. Experts are picking the Cardinals to finish last in their division, if not last in the entire NFL, and that sounds about right to us, too. We're still not convinced Murray has what it takes to be a franchise quarterback, despite Arizona rushing to pay him like one, and we're not convinced the new head coach is a game-changer either. Leaving Cardinals fans with two consolation prizes: a very good shot at the first pick in the 2024 draft, and plenty of time for Murray to study those tapes.

ARIZONA CARDINALS

Arizona Cardinals

eep track of wins and losses (division games in bold)				W/L	TOTAL
Veek 1	Sun, Sep 10	1:00 PM	at Washington Commanders	___	___/___
Veek 2	Sun, Sep 17	4:05 PM	New York Giants	___	___/___
Veek 3	Sun, Sep 24	4:25 PM	Dallas Cowboys	___	___/___
Veek 4	Sun, Oct 1	4:25 PM	**at San Francisco 49ers**	___	___/___
Veek 5	Sun, Oct 8	4:05 PM	Cincinnati Bengals	___	___/___
Veek 6	Sun, Oct 15	4:25 PM	**at Los Angeles Rams**	___	___/___
Veek 7	Sun, Oct 22	4:05 PM	**at Seattle Seahawks**	___	___/___
Veek 8	Sun, Oct 29	4:25 PM	Baltimore Ravens	___	___/___
Veek 9	Sun, Nov 5	1:00 PM	at Cleveland Browns	___	___/___
Veek 10	Sun, Nov 12	4:05 PM	Atlanta Falcons	___	___/___
Veek 11	Sun, Nov 19	1:00 PM	at Houston Texans	___	___/___
Veek 12	Sun, Nov 26	4:05 PM	**Los Angeles Rams**	___	___/___
Veek 13	Sun, Dec 3	1:00 PM	at Pittsburgh Steelers	___	___/___
Veek 14	BYE WEEK				
Veek 15	Sun, Dec 17	4:05 PM	**San Francisco 49ers**	___	___/___
Veek 16	Sun, Dec 24	4:25 PM	at Chicago Bears	___	___/___
Veek 17	Sun, Dec 31	1:00 PM	at Philadelphia Eagles	___	___/___
Veek 18	Sun, Jan 7	TBD	**Seattle Seahawks**	___	___/___

END OF SEASON RECORD:___/___

DIVISION TOTAL WIN/LOSS: ___/___

ATLANTA FALCONS

Head Coach: Arthur Smith | 2022 Record: 7-10

First Round Draft Pick: Bijan Robinson, RB (8)

While we like Arthur Smith as the head coach, the Falcons still need a convincing leader on the field, and we're just not sure who that might be. The coaches believe in second-year QB Desmond Ridder, and they didn't really have a better option in free agency or the draft, so it's hard to point fingers. Ridder should be helped by a surprisingly good offensive line, ranked by most in the top 10 for 2022, as well as drafting a superb running back at #8. But selecting an elite RB as a top 10 pick (can anyone say Zeke Elliott? Saquon Barkley?) has not proven to be a reliable path to post-season dominance in the past ten years. Meanwhile, Atlanta's defense needs... some work. They ranked a poor 27 out of 32 for overall defense last year, and despite the signing of some decent free agents on the defense, plus a new Defensive Coordinator, we are not convinced the Falcons have made enough improvements during the offseason to truly compete for the NFC South.

ATLANTA FALCONS

TEAM SCHEDULE
Atlanta Falcons

Keep track of wins and losses **(division games in bold)**

				W/L	TOTAL
Week 1	Sun, Sep 10	1:00 PM	**Carolina Panthers**	___	___/___
Week 2	Sun, Sep 17	1:00 PM	Green Bay Packers	___	___/___
Week 3	Sun, Sep 24	1:00 PM	at Detroit Lions	___	___/___
Week 4	Sun, Oct 1	9:30 AM	Jacksonville Jaguars*	___	___/___
Week 5	Sun, Oct 8	1:00 PM	Houston Texans	___	___/___
Week 6	Sun, Oct 15	1:00 PM	Washington Commanders	___	___/___
Week 7	Sun, Oct 22	1:00 PM	**at Tampa Bay Buccaneers**	___	___/___
Week 8	Sun, Oct 29	1:00 PM	at Tennessee Titans	___	___/___
Week 9	Sun, Nov 5	1:00 PM	Minnesota Vikings	___	___/___
Week 10	Sun, Nov 12	4:05 PM	at Arizona Cardinals	___	___/___
Week 11	BYE WEEK				
Week 12	Sun, Nov 26	1:00 PM	**New Orleans Saints**	___	___/___
Week 13	Sun, Dec 3	1:00 PM	at New York Jets	___	___/___
Week 14	Sun, Dec 10	1:00 PM	**Tampa Bay Buccaneers**	___	___/___
Week 15	Sun, Dec 17	TBD	at Carolina Panthers	___	___/___
Week 16	Sun, Dec 24	1:00 PM	Indianapolis Colts	___	___/___
Week 17	Sun, Dec 31	1:00 PM	at Chicago Bears	___	___/___
Week 18	Sun, Jan 7	TBD	**at New Orleans Saints**	___	___/___

END OF SEASON RECORD:___/___

*international game

DIVISION TOTAL WIN/LOSS: ___/___

BALTIMORE RAVENS

Head Coach: John Harbaugh | 2022 Record: 10-7

First Round Draft Pick: Zay Flowers, WR (22)

Gentlemen, we have a deal. Thanks to persistence and unflagging good faith on both sides, the Ravens will start the 2023 season with their franchise quarterback freshly signed to a monster new deal, and free from any distractions that might keep him from reaching his full potential. And make no mistake, we believe Lamar has not hit his ceiling. Which is excellent news for Ravens fans. Baltimore's front office has loaded up on weapons for their QB, including Odell Beckham Jr., Nelson Agular, and their first-round pick, Zay Flowers. Add those names to WR Rashad Bateman and TE Marc Andrews, and Lamar should have plenty of options down the field. We love this head coach, and believe in this organization, so we are keeping the Ravens in the playoff hunt, despite a very tough divisional rival in Cincinnati, not to mention a brutal landscape in the AFC.

BALTIMORE RAVENS

TEAM SCHEDULE
Baltimore Ravens

			Keep track of wins and losses (division games in bold)	W/L	TOTAL
Week 1	Sun, Sep 10	1:00 PM	Houston Texans	___	___/___
Week 2	Sun, Sep 17	1:00 PM	**at Cincinnati Bengals**	___	___/___
Week 3	Sun, Sep 24	1:00 PM	Indianapolis Colts	___	___/___
Week 4	Sun, Oct 1	1:00 PM	**at Cleveland Browns**	___	___/___
Week 5	Sun, Oct 8	1:00 PM	**at Pittsburgh Steelers**	___	___/___
Week 6	Sun, Oct 15	9:30 AM	Tennessee Titans*	___	___/___
Week 7	Sun, Oct 22	1:00 PM	Detroit Lions	___	___/___
Week 8	Sun, Oct 29	4:25 PM	at Arizona Cardinals	___	___/___
Week 9	Sun, Nov 5	1:00 PM	Seattle Seahawks	___	___/___
Week 10	Sun, Nov 12	1:00 PM	**Cleveland Browns**	___	___/___
Week 11	Thu, Nov 16	8:15 PM	**Cincinnati Bengals**	___	___/___
Week 12	Sun, Nov 26	8:20 PM	at Los Angeles Chargers	___	___/___
Week 13	BYE WEEK				
Week 14	Sun, Dec 10	1:00 PM	Los Angeles Rams	___	___/___
Week 15	Sun, Dec 17	8:20 PM	at Jacksonville Jaguars	___	___/___
Week 16	Mon, Dec 25	8:15 PM	at San Francisco 49ers	___	___/___
Week 17	Sun, Dec 31	1:00 PM	Miami Dolphins	___	___/___
Week 18	Sun, Jan 7	TBD	**Pittsburgh Steelers**	___	___/___

END OF SEASON RECORD:___/___

*International game

DIVISION TOTAL WIN/LOSS: ___/___

BUFFALO BILLS

Head Coach: Sean McDermott | 2022 Record: 13-3
First Round Draft Pick: Dalton Kincaid, TE (25)

The world held its breath as a scene unfolded in Buffalo unlike anything we've seen on national football TV. As emergency responders saved a young man's life right before our eyes, players on both teams staggered, cried, and comforted each other. My favorite visual was Joe Burrow walking across the field to put his arm around Josh Allen, as the Buffalo QB struggled to cope with the enormity of the unfolding crisis. That said everything about the game I love. No matter what team you root for, we all celebrated Damar Hamlin's miraculous recovery, as we are reminded how important (and talented) are the medical crews on the sidelines. But the Bills looked shell-shocked for the rest of the season. They stumbled in the play-offs, losing to Cincinnati in the divisional round, and sitting at home while their two biggest rivals fought it out for the AFC Championship. Trouble is, Kansas City and Cincinnati aren't going anywhere. But you know who did go somewhere? Aaron Rodgers. With Rodgers at the Jets, and Miami stacked with speed, the Bills division is getting tougher. We are fans of Josh Allen and his coach, Sean McDermott, but Buffalo may have missed their best opportunity to hoist the Lombardi.

BUFFALO BILLS

TEAM SCHEDULE
Buffalo Bills

eep track of wins and losses *(division games in bold)*				W/L	TOTAL
Week 1	Mon, Sep 11	8:15 PM	**at New York Jets**	___	___/___
Week 2	Sun, Sep 17	1:00 PM	Las Vegas Raiders	___	___/___
Week 3	Sun, Sep 24	1:00 PM	at Washington Commanders	___	___/___
Week 4	Sun, Oct 1	1:00 PM	**Miami Dolphins**	___	___/___
Week 5	Sun, Oct 8	9:30 AM	Jacksonville Jaguars*	___	___/___
Week 6	Sun, Oct 15	8:20 PM	New York Giants	___	___/___
Week 7	Sun, Oct 22	1:00 PM	**at New England Patriots**	___	___/___
Week 8	Thu, Oct 26	8:15 PM	Tampa Bay Buccaneers	___	___/___
Week 9	Sun, Nov 5	8:20 PM	at Cincinnati Bengals	___	___/___
Week 10	Mon, Nov 13	8:15 PM	Denver Broncos	___	___/___
Week 11	Sun, Nov 19	4:25 PM	**New York Jets**	___	___/___
Week 12	Sun, Nov 26	4:25 PM	at Philadelphia Eagles	___	___/___
Week 13	BYE WEEK				
Week 14	Sun, Dec 10	4:25 PM	at Kansas City Chiefs	___	___/___
Week 15	Sun, Dec 17	4:25 PM	Dallas Cowboys	___	___/___
Week 16	Sat, Dec 23	8:00 PM	at Los Angeles Chargers	___	___/___
Week 17	Sun, Dec 31	1:00 PM	**New England Patriots**	___	___/___
Week 18	Sun, Jan 7	TBD	**at Miami Dolphins**	___	___/___

END OF SEASON RECORD:___/___

*international game

DIVISION TOTAL WIN/LOSS: ___/___

CAROLINA PANTHERS

Head Coach: Frank Reich* | 2022 Record: 7-10
First Round Draft Pick: Bryce Young, QB (1)

*new head coac

The Panthers had a dismal 2022, but when it came time to turn the page, they didn't mess around. They hired Frank Reich to be their new head coach, and then traded all the way up to #1 to draft their future franchise quarterback. At least, that's the idea. When you watch the tape, Bryce Young looks amazing — perfect passing accuracy, outstanding situational awareness, great arm strength. But does his helmet look a little big for his head? I mean, he's just not a big guy. And when Aaron Donald or Myles Garrett or Nick Bosa or Hassan Reddick charge like an angry bull, the Panther's new #1 pick might just get flattened. Still, there's no question that Carolina's offense has improved, not just with a new HC and QB, but also with the addition of TE Hayden Hurst. Carolina's defense, unfortunately, was nothing to write home about in 2022 and it didn't improve much this offseason. Yes, the Panthers play in a fairly weak division in the weaker of the two conferences. Still, they have a lot of work ahead before they can be considered play-off material.

CAROLINA PANTHERS

Carolina Panthers

Keep track of wins and losses (division games in bold)				W/L	TOTAL
Week 1	Sun, Sep 10	1:00 PM	**at Atlanta Falcons**	___	___/___
Week 2	Mon, Sep 18	7:15 PM	**New Orleans Saints**	___	___/___
Week 3	Sun, Sep 24	4:05 PM	at Seattle Seahawks	___	___/___
Week 4	Sun, Oct 1	1:00 PM	Minnesota Vikings	___	___/___
Week 5	Sun, Oct 8	1:00 PM	at Detroit Lions	___	___/___
Week 6	Sun, Oct 15	1:00 PM	at Miami Dolphins	___	___/___
Week 7	BYE WEEK				
Week 8	Sun, Oct 29	1:00 PM	Houston Texans	___	___/___
Week 9	Sun, Nov 5	4:05 PM	Indianapolis Colts	___	___/___
Week 10	Thu, Nov 9	8:15 PM	at Chicago Bears	___	___/___
Week 11	Sun, Nov 19	1:00 PM	Dallas Cowboys	___	___/___
Week 12	Sun, Nov 26	1:00 PM	at Tennessee Titans	___	___/___
Week 13	Sun, Dec 3	1:00 PM	**at Tampa Bay Buccaneers**	___	___/___
Week 14	Sun, Dec 10	1:00 PM	**at New Orleans Saints**	___	___/___
Week 15	Sun, Dec 17	TBD	**Atlanta Falcons**	___	___/___
Week 16	Sun, Dec 24	1:00 PM	Green Bay Packers	___	___/___
Week 17	Sun, Dec 31	1:00 PM	at Jacksonville Jaguars	___	___/___
Week 18	Sun, Jan 7	TBD	**Tampa Bay Buccaneers**	___	___/___

END OF SEASON RECORD:___/___

DIVISION TOTAL WIN/LOSS: ___/___

CHICAGO BEARS

Head Coach: Matt Eberflus | 2022 Record: 3-14
First Round Draft Pick: Darnell Wright, OT (10)

We still believe in you, Justin Fields! You've faced some stiff headwinds in your first two years, but you made progress and we hope you are on a Lamar Jackson (if not Josh Allen) path of improvement. And we join you in appreciating the first round pick of an offensive tackle to help you stay upright and in the pocket. Assuming you are actually in the pocket. *Ever*. Because, to get to that next level, you have to pass more and rush less. Here are two stats that tell you everything you need to know: Chicago ranked 29th (out of 32) in passing yards for 2022, but they ranked #1 for rushing yards. You know why? Because Justin Fields was rushing instead of passing. In fact, Fields was the team's #1 rusher. By a long shot. What's the problem, you say — yards are yards, right? Well, Chicago also ranked 28th in total yards gained per game. So unless the Bears want to move him to running back and bring in another quarterback, Chicago has to get Fields to Throw. The. Ball. Meanwhile, new HC Matt Eberflus will have plenty of "opportunities" to strengthen the defensive side of the ball, as Chicago gave up more points per game than any other team in the NFL last year. Suffice it to say, the Bears have a steep uphill climb ahead of them.

CHICAGO BEARS

Chicago Bears

			keep track of wins and losses (division games in bold)	W/L	TOTAL
Week 1	Sun, Sep 10	4:25 PM	**Green Bay Packers**	___	___/___
Week 2	Sun, Sep 17	1:00 PM	at Tampa Bay Buccaneers	___	___/___
Week 3	Sun, Sep 24	4:25 PM	at Kansas City Chiefs	___	___/___
Week 4	Sun, Oct 1	1:00 PM	Denver Broncos	___	___/___
Week 5	Thu, Oct 5	8:15 PM	at Washington Commanders	___	___/___
Week 6	Sun, Oct 15	1:00 PM	**Minnesota Vikings**	___	___/___
Week 7	Sun, Oct 22	1:00 PM	Las Vegas Raiders	___	___/___
Week 8	Sun, Oct 29	8:20 PM	at Los Angeles Chargers	___	___/___
Week 9	Sun, Nov 5	1:00 PM	at New Orleans Saints	___	___/___
Week 10	Thu, Nov 9	8:15 PM	Carolina Panthers	___	___/___
Week 11	Sun, Nov 19	1:00 PM	**at Detroit Lions**	___	___/___
Week 12	Mon, Nov 27	8:15 PM	**at Minnesota Vikings**	___	___/___
Week 13	BYE WEEK				
Week 14	Sun, Dec 10	1:00 PM	**Detroit Lions**	___	___/___
Week 15	Sun, Dec 17	TBD	at Cleveland Browns	___	___/___
Week 16	Sun, Dec 24	4:25 PM	Arizona Cardinals	___	___/___
Week 17	Sun, Dec 31	1:00 PM	Atlanta Falcons	___	___/___
Week 18	Sun, Jan 7	TBD	**at Green Bay Packers**	___	___/___

END OF SEASON RECORD:___/___

DIVISION TOTAL WIN/LOSS: ___/___

CINCINNATI BENGALS

Head Coach: Zac Taylor | 2022 Record: 12-4

First Round Draft Pick: Myles Murphy, Edge (28)

If anyone still had doubts about Joe Burrow entering last season, those are g-o-n-e gone. Getting to the Super Bowl was no fluke, and plenty of fans think they were a heartbeat away from getting there again. Pun intended. By playing one fewer game, they never got the chance to secure home field advantage in the AFC championship, and then a couple questionable penalties kept them from beating the Chiefs anyway. We expect the Bengals to be in the hunt for the Super Bowl for many years to come. Like Burrow said, their window is his career. It's not just Burrow that has us bullish on the Bengals. In addition to being top 5 in passing (yards per game), total touchdowns, and completion percentage, Cincinnati was also top 10 in total yards per game and 5th in points per game (tied w Dallas). The Bengals' front office did an excellent job in coping with a challenging offseason; while they lost TE Hayden Hurst, they signed TE Irv Smith Jr., and while they lost both their safeties Von Bell and Jessie Bates, they added an outstanding offensive lineman in tackle Orlando Brown (making rival Kansas City's O-line a bit weaker in the process). Overall, the Bengals look poised for another deep playoff run.

CINCINNATI BENGALS

TEAM SCHEDULE
Cincinnati Bengals

Keep track of wins and losses **(division games in bold)**

				W/L	TOTAL
Week 1	Sun, Sep 10	1:00 PM	**at Cleveland Browns**	___	___/___
Week 2	Sun, Sep 17	1:00 PM	**Baltimore Ravens**	___	___/___
Week 3	Mon, Sep 25	8:15 PM	Los Angeles Rams	___	___/___
Week 4	Sun, Oct 1	1:00 PM	at Tennessee Titans	___	___/___
Week 5	Sun, Oct 8	4:05 PM	at Arizona Cardinals	___	___/___
Week 6	Sun, Oct 15	1:00 PM	Seattle Seahawks	___	___/___
Week 7	BYE WEEK				
Week 8	Sun, Oct 29	4:25 PM	at San Francisco 49ers	___	___/___
Week 9	Sun, Nov 5	8:20 PM	Buffalo Bills	___	___/___
Week 10	Sun, Nov 12	1:00 PM	Houston Texans	___	___/___
Week 11	Thu, Nov 16	8:15 PM	**at Baltimore Ravens**	___	___/___
Week 12	Sun, Nov 26	1:00 PM	**Pittsburgh Steelers**	___	___/___
Week 13	Mon, Dec 4	8:15 PM	at Jacksonville Jaguars	___	___/___
Week 14	Sun, Dec 10	1:00 PM	Indianapolis Colts	___	___/___
Week 15	Sun, Dec 17	TBD	Minnesota Vikings	___	___/___
Week 16	Sat, Dec 23	4:30 PM	**at Pittsburgh Steelers**	___	___/___
Week 17	Sun, Dec 31	4:25 PM	at Kansas City Chiefs	___	___/___
Week 18	Sun, Jan 7	TBD	**Cleveland Browns**	___	___/___

END OF SEASON RECORD:___/___

DIVISION TOTAL WIN/LOSS: ___/___

Can you say "dark horse playoff team?" With the AFC loaded with talent, it's hard for even the **proven** teams to punch their ticket to the playoffs. So not many pundits are picking the Browns to be playing in the post-season. But we remember Deshaun Watson when he played in Houston. He was often extraordinary and sometimes miraculous. Has that just gone away? The fact is, we just don't know. Meanwhile, Cleveland is stacked with talent on aboth sides of the ball, from Myles Garrett (#2 in total sacks last year) to Nick Chubb, Amari Cooper, ZeDarius Smith, Dalvin Tomlinson and Elijah Moore. We also love the hiring of new defensive coordinator, Jim Schwartz (**didn't** love him as a head coach, **do** love him as a DC). So, despite a mediocre record in 2022, and middle-of-the-pack performance (ranking 14th in both overall defense and overall offense), this team could just surprise us in 2023. It would be mighty fun to watch — and high time for Stefanski to prove he is an elite head coach.

TEAM SCHEDULE
Cleveland Browns

Keep track of wins and losses (division games in bold)				W/L	TOTAL
Week 1	Sun, Sep 10	1:00 PM	**Cincinnati Bengals**	___	___/___
Week 2	Mon, Sep 18	8:15 PM	**at Pittsburgh Steelers**	___	___/___
Week 3	Sun, Sep 24	1:00 PM	Tennessee Titans	___	___/___
Week 4	Sun, Oct 1	1:00 PM	**Baltimore Ravens**	___	___/___
Week 5	BYE WEEK				
Week 6	Sun, Oct 15	1:00 PM	San Francisco 49ers	___	___/___
Week 7	Sun, Oct 22	1:00 PM	at Indianapolis Colts	___	___/___
Week 8	Sun, Oct 29	4:05 PM	at Seattle Seahawks	___	___/___
Week 9	Sun, Nov 5	1:00 PM	Arizona Cardinals	___	___/___
Week 10	Sun, Nov 12	1:00 PM	**at Baltimore Ravens**	___	___/___
Week 11	Sun, Nov 19	1:00 PM	**Pittsburgh Steelers**	___	___/___
Week 12	Sun, Nov 26	4:05 PM	at Denver Broncos	___	___/___
Week 13	Sun, Dec 3	4:25 PM	at Los Angeles Rams	___	___/___
Week 14	Sun, Dec 10	1:00 PM	Jacksonville Jaguars	___	___/___
Week 15	Sun, Dec 17	TBD	Chicago Bears	___	___/___
Week 16	Sun, Dec 24	1:00 PM	at Houston Texans	___	___/___
Week 17	Thu, Dec 28	8:15 PM	New York Jets	___	___/___
Week 18	Sun, Jan 7	TBD	**at Cincinnati Bengals**	___	___/___

END OF SEASON RECORD:___/___

DIVISION TOTAL WIN/LOSS: ___/___

DALLAS COWBOYS

Head Coach: Mike McCarthy | 2022 Record: 12-5
First Round Draft Pick: Mazi Smith, DT (26)

The Cowboys delighted their fans with an offense that was top-10 overall and top-4 in scoring across the entire NFL. Unfortunately, fans were also treated to 15 interceptions, the highest rate of any starting QB last year. Worse yet, Dallas fans watched their Cowboys score a paltry 12 points in their playoff loss to the 49ers, ending what looked to be another promising season. Sacrificial lamb? We offer you: Offensive coordinator Kellen Moore. We were never huge Kellen Moore fans, tainted perhaps by his years under HC Jason Garrett, but moving the play-calling duties to Mike McCarthy doesn't exactly increase our confidence. Nor does the loss of their outstanding TE Dalton Schultz. (We are very glad that Dallas' excellent defensive coordinator, Dan Quinn is still at the helm, though.) The question remains the same as it's been for several years now: what will take the Cowboys from playoff team to Super Bowl champ? That answer has to come from Dak.

DALLAS COWBOYS

TEAM SCHEDULE
Dallas Cowboys

keep track of wins and losses (division games in bold)				W/L	TOTAL
Week 1	Sun, Sep 10	8:20 PM	**at New York Giants**	___	___/___
Week 2	Sun, Sep 17	4:25 PM	New York Jets	___	___/___
Week 3	Sun, Sep 24	4:25 PM	at Arizona Cardinals	___	___/___
Week 4	Sun, Oct 1	4:25 PM	New England Patriots	___	___/___
Week 5	Sun, Oct 8	8:20 PM	at San Francisco 49ers	___	___/___
Week 6	Mon, Oct 16	8:15 PM	at Los Angeles Chargers	___	___/___
Week 7	BYE WEEK				
Week 8	Sun, Oct 29	1:00 PM	Los Angeles Rams	___	___/___
Week 9	Sun, Nov 5	4:25 PM	**at Philadelphia Eagles**	___	___/___
Week 10	Sun, Nov 12	4:25 PM	**New York Giants**	___	___/___
Week 11	Sun, Nov 19	1:00 PM	at Carolina Panthers	___	___/___
Week 12	Thu, Nov 23	4:30 PM	**Washington Commanders**	___	___/___
Week 13	Thu, Nov 30	8:15 PM	Seattle Seahawks	___	___/___
Week 14	Sun, Dec 10	8:20 PM	**Philadelphia Eagles**	___	___/___
Week 15	Sun, Dec 17	4:25 PM	at Buffalo Bills	___	___/___
Week 16	Sun, Dec 24	4:25 PM	at Miami Dolphins	___	___/___
Week 17	Sat, Dec 30	8:15 PM	Detroit Lions	___	___/___
Week 18	Sun, Jan 7	TBD	**at Washington Commanders**	___	___/___

END OF SEASON RECORD: ___/___

DIVISION TOTAL WIN/LOSS: ___/___

DENVER BRONCOS

Head Coach: Sean Payton* | 2022 Record: 5-12
First Round Draft Pick: No Picks in Round 1

*new head coa

Denver took us by surprise last season, and not in a good way. We didn't actually think Russell Wilson could be *that* bad. Sure, Nathaniel Hackett was a disaster as head coach, but still... can all the Broncos' woes be blamed on him? I guess we will see. Enter Sean Payton, the most sought-after coach in all of the NFL this past off-season. Payton got to work immediately, installing Joe Lombardi as the new Offensive Coordinator, Vance Joseph as the new Defensive Coordinator, and a new "time to get serious" attitude throughout the building. Russell Wilson says goodbye to his personal training staff, and we look forward to a much more disciplined team taking the field at Mile High Stadium. Jerry Jeudy, Frank Clark, Mike McGlinchey, Courtland Sutton, Patrick Surtain, Justin Simmons — there are enough quality players here to take this team seriously. If Wilson can return to form, that is.

DENVER BRONCOS

TEAM SCHEDULE
Denver Broncos

				W/L	TOTAL
eep track of wins and losses **(division games in bold)**					
Week 1	Sun, Sep 10	4:25 PM	**Las Vegas Raiders**	___	___/___
Week 2	Sun, Sep 17	4:25 PM	Washington Commanders	___	___/___
Week 3	Sun, Sep 24	1:00 PM	at Miami Dolphins	___	___/___
Week 4	Sun, Oct 1	1:00 PM	at Chicago Bears	___	___/___
Week 5	Sun, Oct 8	4:25 PM	New York Jets	___	___/___
Week 6	Thu, Oct 12	8:15 PM	**at Kansas City Chiefs**	___	___/___
Week 7	Sun, Oct 22	4:25 PM	Green Bay Packers	___	___/___
Week 8	Sun, Oct 29	4:25 PM	**Kansas City Chiefs**	___	___/___
Week 9	BYE WEEK				
Week 10	Mon, Nov 13	8:15 PM	at Buffalo BIlls	___	___/___
Week 11	Sun, Nov 19	8:20 PM	Minnesota Vikings	___	___/___
Week 12	Sun, Nov 26	4:05 PM	Cleveland Browns	___	___/___
Week 13	Sun, Dec 3	4:05 PM	at Houston Texans	___	___/___
Week 14	Sun, Dec 10	4:25 PM	**at Los Angeles Chargers**	___	___/___
Week 15	Sun, Dec 17	TBD	at Detroit Lions	___	___/___
Week 16	Sun, Dec 24	8:15 PM	New England Patriots	___	___/___
Week 17	Sun, Dec 31	4:25 PM	**Los Angeles Chargers**	___	___/___
Week 18	Sun, Jan 7	TBD	**at Las Vegas Raiders**	___	___/___

END OF SEASON RECORD:___/___

DIVISION TOTAL WIN/LOSS: ___/___

DETROIT LIONS

Head Coach: Dan Campbell | 2022 Record: 9-8

First Round Draft Pick: Jahmyr Gibbs, RB (12); Jack Campell, LB (18)

Who's laughing at kneecaps now? Dan Campbell has turned the Lions into a tough, determined and very dangerous team, as the Green Bay Packers learned last season. Even after they were eliminated from play-off competition, the Lions grit their teeth, rubbed a little dirt on their uniforms, and beat Aaron Rodgers in his last game as a Packer. Detroit's motto entering the game: "Either we go to the playoffs or they don't." You gotta love that. As they enter 2023, the biggest change Detroit made is to their secondary, bringing in a trio of impressive new faces: Cameron Sutton, C.J. Gardner-Johnson and Emmanuel Moseley. They kept their excellent wide receiver, Aman-Ra St. Brown (#7 among all pass catchers in the league last year), but lost their top rusher, Jamaal Williams. Which is perhaps why they chose Gibbs so high in the first round of the draft. All told, Detroit looks as strong as last year, but with more experience and confidence under their belt. Now that they've run Aaron Rodgers out of town, the NFC North could actually be up for grabs. Why not the Lions?

DETROIT LIONS

Detroit Lions

Keep track of wins and losses (*division games in bold*)				W/L	TOTAL
Week 1	Thu, Sep 7	8:20 PM	at Kansas City Chiefs	___	___/___
Week 2	Sun, Sep 17	1:00 PM	Seattle Seahawks	___	___/___
Week 3	Sun, Sep 24	1:00 PM	Atlanta Falcons	___	___/___
Week 4	Thu, Sep 28	8:15 PM	**at Green Bay Packers**	___	___/___
Week 5	Sun, Oct 8	1:00 PM	Carolina Panthers	___	___/___
Week 6	Sun, Oct 15	1:00 PM	at Tampa Bay Buccaneers	___	___/___
Week 7	Sun, Oct 22	1:00 PM	at Baltimore Ravens	___	___/___
Week 8	Mon, Oct 30	8:15 PM	Las Vegas Raiders	___	___/___
Week 9	BYE WEEK				
Week 10	Sun, Nov 12	4:05 PM	at Los Angeles Chargers	___	___/___
Week 11	Sun, Nov 19	1:00 PM	**Chicago Bears**	___	___/___
Week 12	Thu, Nov 23	12:30 PM	**Green Bay Packers**	___	___/___
Week 13	Sun, Dec 3	1:00 PM	at New Orleans Saints	___	___/___
Week 14	Sun, Dec 10	1:00 PM	**at Chicago Bears**	___	___/___
Week 15	Sun, Dec 17	TBD	Denver Broncos	___	___/___
Week 16	Sun, Dec 24	1:00 PM	**at Minnesota Vikings**	___	___/___
Week 17	Sat, Dec 30	8:15 PM	at Dallas Cowboys	___	___/___
Week 18	Sun, Jan 7	TBD	**Minnesota Vikings**	___	___/___

END OF SEASON RECORD: ___/___

DIVISION TOTAL WIN/LOSS: ___/___

GREEN BAY PACKERS

Head Coach: Matt LaFleur | 2022 Record: 8-9

First Round Draft Pick: Lukas Van Ness, Edge (13)

It looks like the schedulers forgot that Aaron Rodgers is no longer the quarterback of the Green Bay Packers. The team will play in *five* prime time games this season, not counting Thanksgiving Day, giving all of us a really good look at.... Jordan Love? The Packers' best player might still be named Aaron, but when your best player is not your quarterback, you could be staring another losing season in the face. Green Bay just wasn't that impressive last year, and without their future Hall-of-Fame QB behind center. we are not convinced they will be contenders, even in the weak NFC.

GREEN BAY PACKERS

Green Bay Packers

eep track of wins and losses **(division games in bold)**

				W/L	TOTAL
Week 1	Sun, Sep 10	4:25 PM	**at Chicago Bears**	___	___/___
Week 2	Sun, Sep 17	1:00 PM	at Atlanta Falcons	___	___/___
Week 3	Sun, Sep 24	1:00 PM	New Orleans Saints	___	___/___
Week 4	Thu, Sep 28	8:15 PM	**Detroit Lions**	___	___/___
Week 5	Mon, Oct 9	8:15 PM	at Las Vegas Raiders	___	___/___
Week 6	BYE WEEK				
Week 7	Sun, Oct 22	4:25 PM	at Denver Broncos	___	___/___
Week 8	Sun, Oct 29	1:00 PM	**Minnesota Vikings**	___	___/___
Week 9	Sun, Nov 5	1:00 PM	Los Angeles Rams	___	___/___
Week 10	Sun, Nov 12	1:00 PM	at Pittsburgh Steelers	___	___/___
Week 11	Sun, Nov 19	1:00 PM	Los Angeles Chargers	___	___/___
Week 12	Thu, Nov. 23	12:30 PM	**at Detroit Lions**	___	___/___
Week 13	Sun, Dec 3	8:20 PM	Kansas City Chiefs	___	___/___
Week 14	Mon, Dec 11	8:15 PM	at New York Giants	___	___/___
Week 15	Sun, Dec 17	1:00 PM	Tampa Bay Buccaneers	___	___/___
Week 16	Sun, Dec 24	1:00 PM	at Carolina Panthers	___	___/___
Week 17	Sun, Dec 31	8:20 PM	**at Minnesota Vikings**	___	___/___
Week 18	Sun, Jan 7	TBD	**Chicago Bears**	___	___/___

END OF SEASON RECORD:___/___

DIVISION TOTAL WIN/LOSS: ___/___

HOUSTON TEXANS

Head Coach: DeMeco Ryan* | 2022 Record: 3-13-1
First Round Draft Pick: C. J. Stroud, QB (2); Will Anderson Jr, Edge (3)

*new head coa

He proved himself a brilliant defensive coordinator in San Francisco. Now DeMeco Ryan has a much bigger challenge: to rescue the Texans from a downward spiral of their own making. A promising new head coach + a promising rookie quarterback = a good start. We loved their draft-day maneuver to snag both their future franchise quarterback and the best defensive player in the draft. We also like the signing of TE Dalton Schultz and LB Denzel Perryman Iit will probably take some time for all the pieces to come together, and for Houston to make noise in the crowded AFC, but we like the direction of this team.

HOUSTON TEXANS

TEAM SCHEDULE
Houston Texans

				W/L	TOTAL
*eep track of wins and losses **(division games in bold)***					
Week 1	Sun, Sep 10	1:00 PM	at Baltimore Ravens	___	___/___
Week 2	Sun, Sep 17	1:00 PM	**Indianapolis Colts**	___	___/___
Week 3	Sun, Sep 24	1:00 PM	**at Jacksonville Jaguars**	___	___/___
Week 4	Sun, Oct 1	1:00 PM	Pittsburgh Steelers	___	___/___
Week 5	Sun, Oct 8	1:00 PM	at Atlanta Falcons	___	___/___
Week 6	Sun, Oct 15	1:00 PM	New Orleans Saints	___	___/___
Week 7	BYE WEEK				
Week 8	Sun, Oct 29	1:00 PM	at Carolina Panthers	___	___/___
Week 9	Sun, Nov 5	1:00 PM	Tampa Bay Buccaneers	___	___/___
Week 10	Sun, Nov 12	1:00 PM	at Cincinnati Bengals	___	___/___
Week 11	Sun, Nov 19	1:00 PM	Arizona Cardinals	___	___/___
Week 12	Sun, Nov 26	1:00 PM	**Jacksonville Jaguars**	___	___/___
Week 13	Sun, Dec 3	4:05 PM	Denver Broncos	___	___/___
Week 14	Sun, Dec 10	1:00 PM	at New York Jets	___	___/___
Week 15	Sun, Dec 17	1:00 PM	**at Tennessee Titans**	___	___/___
Week 16	Sun, Dec 24	1:00 PM	Cleveland Browns	___	___/___
Week 17	Sun, Dec 31	1:00 PM	**Tennessee Titans**	___	___/___
Week 18	Sun, Jan 7	TBD	**at Indianapolis Colts**	___	___/___

END OF SEASON RECORD:___/___

DIVISION TOTAL WIN/LOSS: ___/___

INDIANAPOLIS COLTS

Head Coach: Shane Steichen* | 2022 Record: 4-12-1

First Round Draft Pick: Anthony Richardson, QB (4)

*new head coa

Old guys, stand aside. Retreads, move along. Make way for the next generation of the Indianapolis Colts. We believe it took the Colts several years to come to terms with the surprise early retirement of Andrew Luck, as they kept trying to plug in cast-off quarterbacks in his place. Now, at last, they turn the page, giving fans a new head coach and an exciting new prospect as their potential future franchise quarterback. Everyone knows Anthony Richardson is raw. He played just 19 games in college. He "boasted" a completion percentage below 55% and 14 interceptions vs 23 touchdowns. But his physical gifts are awesome and his attitude is exactly what you want: he knows he needs to learn and he's ready to do it. Which is one reason Shane Steichen is such a perfect fit at head coach. After helping Jalen Hurts go from question mark (87.2 passer rating his rookie year) to exclamation point (101 passer rating last year), Steichen is exactly what the doctor ordered for Indy's #4 overall pick. Add to that their outstanding RB, Jonathan Taylor (excused for a down year in 2022 due to ankle injury), and their top-10 WR, Michael Pittman Jr., Indy has talent. The question for Colts fans in 2023 is this: when Gardner Minshew makes way for Anthony Richardson, will the new QB be ready for prime time?

INDIANAPOLIS COLTS

TEAM SCHEDULE
Indianapolis Colts

Keep track of wins and losses *(division games in bold)*				W/L	TOTAL
Week 1	Sun, Sep 10	1:00 PM	**Jacksonville Jaguars**	___	___/___
Week 2	Sun, Sep 17	1:00 PM	**at Houston Texans**	___	___/___
Week 3	Sun, Sep 24	1:00 PM	at Baltimore Ravens	___	___/___
Week 4	Sun, Oct 1	1:00 PM	Los Angeles Rams	___	___/___
Week 5	Sun, Oct 8	1:00 PM	**Tennessee Titans**	___	___/___
Week 6	Sun, Oct 15	1:00 PM	**at Jacksonville Jaguars**	___	___/___
Week 7	Sun, Oct 22	1:00 PM	Cleveland Browns	___	___/___
Week 8	Sun, Oct 29	1:00 PM	New Orleans Saints	___	___/___
Week 9	Sun, Nov 5	4:05 PM	at Carolina Panthers	___	___/___
Week 10	Sun, Nov 12	9:30 AM	New England Patriots*	___	___/___
Week 11	BYE WEEK				
Week 12	Sun, Nov 26	1:00 PM	Tampa Bay Buccaneers	___	___/___
Week 13	Sun, Dec 3	1:00 PM	**Tennessee Titans**	___	___/___
Week 14	Sun, Dec 10	1:00 PM	at Cincinnati Bengals	___	___/___
Week 15	Sun, Dec 17	TBD	Pittsburgh Steelers	___	___/___
Week 16	Sun, Dec 24	1:00 PM	at Atlanta Falcons	___	___/___
Week 17	Sun, Dec 31	1:00 PM	Las Vegas Raiders	___	___/___
Week 18	Sun, Jan 7	TBD	**Houston Texans**	___	___/___

END OF SEASON RECORD:___/___

*international game

DIVISION TOTAL WIN/LOSS: ___/___

JACKSONVILLE JAGUARS

Head Coach: Doug Pederson | 2022 Record: 9-8
First Round Draft Pick: Anton Harrison, OT (27)

Great improvement, great resiliency, great long-ball, really great hair. Trevor Lawrence emerged from the utter dysfunction of his rookie year to become one of the best young quarterbacks in the league. Proving that drafting Lawrence was a very smart move after all. Also proving that the second smartest thing this franchise has done in a long time is hire Doug Pederson as their head coach. With those two pieces in place, this is the year for the Jaguars to prove they are ready to run with the big boys. Beating the Chargers in the Wild Card Round last year said more about the Chargers than the Jags, and overcoming four interceptions is not a habit we'd like to cultivate. Time to clean up the mistakes, lock in and hunt for bear. Or Bengals.

JACKSONVILLE JAGUARS

Jacksonville Jaguars

keep track of wins and losses *(division games in bold)*   **W/L**   **TOTAL**

				W/L	TOTAL
Week 1	Sun, Sep 10	1:00 PM	**at Indianapolis Colts**	___	___/___
Week 2	Sun, Sep 17	1:00 PM	Kansas City Chiefs	___	___/___
Week 3	Sun, Sep 24	1:00 PM	**Houston Texans**	___	___/___
Week 4	Sun, Oct 1	9:30 AM	Atlanta Falcons*	___	___/___
Week 5	Sun, Oct 8	9:30 AM	Buffalo Bills*	___	___/___
Week 6	Sun, Oct 15	1:00 PM	**Indianapolis Colts**	___	___/___
Week 7	Thu, Oct 19	8:15 PM	at New Orleans Saints	___	___/___
Week 8	Sun, Oct 29	1:00 PM	at Pittsburgh Steelers	___	___/___
Week 9	BYE WEEK				
Week 10	Sun, Nov 12	1:00 PM	San Francisco 49ers	___	___/___
Week 11	Sun, Nov 19	1:00 PM	**Tennessee Titans**	___	___/___
Week 12	Sun, Nov 26	1:00 PM	**at Houston Texans**	___	___/___
Week 13	Mon, Dec 4	8:15 PM	Cincinnati Bengals	___	___/___
Week 14	Sun, Dec 10	1:00 PM	at Cleveland Browns	___	___/___
Week 15	Sun, Dec 17	8:20 PM	Baltimore Ravens	___	___/___
Week 16	Sun, Dec 24	4:05 PM	at Tampa Bay Buccaneers	___	___/___
Week 17	Sun, Dec 31	1:00 PM	Carolina Panthers	___	___/___
Week 18	Sun, Jan 7	TBD	**at Tennessee Titans**	___	___/___

END OF SEASON RECORD:___/___

international game

DIVISION TOTAL WIN/LOSS: ___/___

KANSAS CITY CHIEFS

Head Coach: Andy Reid | 2022 Record: 14-3

First Round Draft Pick: Felix Anudike-Uzomah, Edge (31)

What does it take to achieve a dynasty? More than two Super Bowl championships? More than 5 straight years as division winners? Whatever your definition, the Chiefs are on track for dynasty-hood. So, what do they have to worry about, as they enter 2023? Joe Burrow, Josh Allen, Justin Herbert, and Trevor Lawrence? Perhaps. Bigger, faster, tougher edge rushers with their sights focused on Patrick Mahommes? Sure. Better rungames from their biggest competitors? Maybe. Saying goodbye to JuJu Smith-Schuster, Mecole Hardman, Orlando Brown, Andrew Wylie and Frank Clark? I guess so. But KC still has excellent defensive players in Chris Jones and Nick Bolton, as well as exciting young offensive talent in Sky Moore, Kadarius Tony, and Isiah Pacheco (and, of course, the best TE in the league, Travis Kelce). No, the biggest risk for the team with the best quarterback in the league and one of the best coaches in league history is: themselves. Injury, overconfidence, lack of urgency — those are really the only things we can see jeopardizing Kansas City's continued dominance.

KANSAS CITY CHIEFS

Kansas City Chiefs

keep track of wins and losses *(division games in bold)*				W/L	TOTAL
Week 1	Thu, Sep 7	8:20 PM	Detroit Lions	___	___/___
Week 2	Sun, Sep 17	1:00 PM	at Jacksonville Jaguars	___	___/___
Week 3	Sun, Sep 24	4:25 PM	Chicago Bears	___	___/___
Week 4	Sun, Oct 1	8:20 PM	at New York Jets	___	___/___
Week 5	Sun, Oct 8	4:25 PM	at Minnesota Vikings	___	___/___
Week 6	Thu, Oct 12	8:15 PM	**Denver Broncos**	___	___/___
Week 7	Sun, Oct 22	4:25 PM	**Los Angeles Chargers**	___	___/___
Week 8	Sun, Oct 29	4:25 PM	**at Denver Broncos**	___	___/___
Week 9	Sun, Nov 5	9:30 AM	Miami Dolphins*	___	___/___
Week 10	BYE WEEK				
Week 11	Mon, Nov 20	8:15 PM	Philadelphia Eagles	___	___/___
Week 12	Sun, Nov 26	4:25 PM	**at Las Vegas Raiders**	___	___/___
Week 13	Sun, Dec. 3	8:20 PM	at Green Bay Packers	___	___/___
Week 14	Sun, Dec 10	4:25 PM	Buffalo Bills	___	___/___
Week 15	Mon, Dec 18	8:15 PM	at New England Patriots	___	___/___
Week 16	Mon, Dec 25	1:00 PM	**Las Vegas Raiders**	___	___/___
Week 17	Sun, Dec 31	4:25 PM	Cincinnati Bengals	___	___/___
Week 18	Sun, Jan 7	TBD	**at Los Angeles Chargers**	___	___/___

END OF SEASON RECORD:___/___

*international game

DIVISION TOTAL WIN/LOSS: ___/___

LAS VEGAS RAIDERS

Head Coach: Josh McDaniels | 2022 Record: 6-11

First Round Draft Pick: Tyree Wilson, Edge (7)

Don't call us, we'll call you. With that, Derek Carr was sent home, and Raiders fans were left scratching their heads. Carr had been good, not great, but what was the alternative? Aaron Rodgers was clearly not coming to town, and the Raiders were not picking high enough to snag a top QB in the draft. Did Josh McDaniels have Tom Brady up his sleeve? Not exactly. The Raiders signed a different ex-Patriot to the roster, and so Vegas is betting that Jimmy Garopolo can stay healthy long enough to lead them to the playoffs. Personally, we're taking the under.

LAS VEGAS RAIDERS

TEAM SCHEDULE
Las Vegas Raiders

Keep track of wins and losses (division games in bold)				W/L	TOTAL
Week 1	Sun, Sep 10	4:25 PM	**at Denver Broncos**	___	___/___
Week 2	Sun, Sep 17	1:00 PM	at Buffalo Bills	___	___/___
Week 3	Sun, Sep 24	8:20 PM	Pittsburgh Steelers	___	___/___
Week 4	Sun, Oct 1	4:05 PM	**at Los Angeles Chargers**	___	___/___
Week 5	Mon, Oct 9	8:15 PM	Green Bay Packers	___	___/___
Week 6	Sun, Oct 15	4:05 PM	New England Patriots	___	___/___
Week 7	Sun, Oct 22	1:00 PM	at Chicago Bears	___	___/___
Week 8	Mon, Oct 30	8:15 PM	at Detroit Lions	___	___/___
Week 9	Sun, Nov 5	4:25 PM	New York Giants	___	___/___
Week 10	Sun, Nov 12	8:20 PM	New York Jets	___	___/___
Week 11	Sun, Nov 19	1:00 PM	at Miami Dolphins	___	___/___
Week 12	Sun, Nov 26	4:25 PM	**Kansas City Chiefs**	___	___/___
Week 13	BYE WEEK				
Week 14	Sun, Dec 10	4:05 PM	Minnesota Vikings	___	___/___
Week 15	Thu, Dec 14	8:15 PM	**Los Angeles Chargers**	___	___/___
Week 16	Mon, Dec 25	1:00 PM	**at Kansas City Chiefs**	___	___/___
Week 17	Sun, Dec 31	1:00 PM	at Indianapolis Colts	___	___/___
Week 18	Sun, Jan 7	TBD	**Denver Broncos**	___	___/___

END OF SEASON RECORD:___/___

DIVISION TOTAL WIN/LOSS: ___/___

LOS ANGELES CHARGERS

Head Coach: Brandon Staley | 2022 Record: 10-7

First Round Draft Pick: Quentin Johnston, WR (21)

Justin Herbert and the Chargers finally made it to the playoffs (as we predicted in last year's guide), but they failed in such dramatic fashion that it's put a damper on our enthusiasm for 2023. When the opposing quarterback throws *four interceptions in the first half*, you just can't lose that game. So, now what? LA has brought in Kellen Moore as their new offensive coordinator, but we are not convinced that's the answer. We really love this QB, but we continue to worry that he doesn't have enough around him to beat the stiff competition in the AFC. We'd love to be proven wrong.

LOS ANGELES CHARGERS

Los Angeles Chargers

Keep track of wins and losses *(division games in bold)*				W/L	TOTAL
Week 1	Sun, Sep 10	4:25 PM	Miami Dolphins	___	___/___
Week 2	Sun, Sep 17	1:00 PM	at Tennessee Titans	___	___/___
Week 3	Sun, Sep 24	1:00 PM	at Minnesota Vikings	___	___/___
Week 4	Sun, Oct 1	4:05 PM	**Las Vegas Raiders**	___	___/___
Week 5	BYE WEEK				
Week 6	Mon, Oct 16	8:15 PM	Dallas Cowboys	___	___/___
Week 7	Sun, Oct 22	4:25 PM	**at Kansas City Chiefs**	___	___/___
Week 8	Sun, Oct 29	8:20 PM	Chicago Bears	___	___/___
Week 9	Mon, Nov 6	8:15 PM	at New York Jets	___	___/___
Week 10	Sun, Nov 12	4:05 PM	Detroit Lions	___	___/___
Week 11	Sun, Nov 19	1:00 PM	at Green Bay Packers	___	___/___
Week 12	Sun, Nov 26	8:20 PM	Baltimore Ravens	___	___/___
Week 13	Sun, Dec 3	1:00 PM	at New England Patriots	___	___/___
Week 14	Sun, Dec 10	4:25 PM	**Denver Broncos**	___	___/___
Week 15	Thu, Dec 14	8:15 PM	**at Las Vegas Raiders**	___	___/___
Week 16	Sat, Dec 24	8:00 PM	Buffalo Bills	___	___/___
Week 17	Sun, Dec 31	4:25 PM	**at Denver Broncos**	___	___/___
Week 18	Sun, Jan 7	TBD	**Kansas City Chiefs**	___	___/___

END OF SEASON RECORD:___/___

DIVISION TOTAL WIN/LOSS: ___/___

How the mighty have fallen. It seemed like just yesterday, the Rams were hoisting the Lombardi trophy and Sean McVay was the boy genius. Two years later, they laid an egg. Stafford looks like he should seriously consider retirement for the sake of his health, and all those expensive players on one-year contracts are gone. In fact, of the 28 starters from two years ago, only 10 remain on the team. Despite having one of the best head coaches in the league, the Rams appear to be more rebuilding than reloading in 2023. With the 49ers as the clear leaders in this division, we don't expect to see the Rams on the field in February.

LOS ANGELES RAMS

TEAM SCHEDULE
Los Angeles Rams

eep track of wins and losses (division games in bold)				W/L	TOTAL
Week 1	Sun, Sep 10	4:25 PM	**at Seattle Seahawks**	___	___/___
Week 2	Sun, Sep 17	4:05 PM	**San Francisco 49ers**	___	___/___
Week 3	Mon, Sep 25	8:15 PM	at Cincinnati Bengals	___	___/___
Week 4	Sun, Oct 1	1:00 PM	at Indianapolis Colts	___	___/___
Week 5	Sun, Oct 8	4:05 PM	Philadelphia Eagles	___	___/___
Week 6	Sun, Oct 15	4:25 PM	**Arizona Cardinals**	___	___/___
Week 7	Sun, Oct 22	4:05 PM	Pittsburgh Steelers	___	___/___
Week 8	Sun, Oct 29	1:00 PM	at Dallas Cowboys	___	___/___
Week 9	Sun, Nov 5	1:00 PM	at Green Bay Packers	___	___/___
Week 10	BYE WEEK				
Week 11	Sun, Nov 19	4:25 PM	**Seattle Seahawks**	___	___/___
Week 12	Sun, Nov 26	4:05 PM	**at Arizona Cardinals**	___	___/___
Week 13	Sun, Dec 3	4:25 PM	Cleveland Browns	___	___/___
Week 14	Sun, Dec 10	1:00 PM	at Baltimore Ravens	___	___/___
Week 15	Sun, Dec 17	4:05 PM	Washington Commanders	___	___/___
Week 16	Thu, Dec 21	8:15 PM	New Orleans Saints	___	___/___
Week 17	Sun, Dec 31	1:00 PM	at New York Giants	___	___/___
Week 18	Sun, Jan 7	TBD	**at San Francisco 49ers**	___	___/___

END OF SEASON RECORD:___/___

DIVISION TOTAL WIN/LOSS: ___/___

MIAMI DOLPHINS

Head Coach: Mike McDaniel | 2022 Record: 9-8

First Round Draft Pick: No Picks in Round 1

Miami is frisky and exciting. They are built on speed, with burners at both their starting WR's in Tyreek Hill and Jaylen Waddle. The question is simple: can Tua stay healthy? Multiple concussions in a single season are very troubling, and there is real concern about the ethics of letting a young man back on the field who is so prone to head injury. Where do you draw that line? Tua is eager to play, and to make a run for the hyper-competitive AFC East. But with Rodgers at the Jets, and Josh Allen still in Buffalo, plus little confidence that Tua will play all 17 games, we are worried that the Dolphins won't weather the storm.

MIAMI DOLPHINS

TEAM SCHEDULE
Miami Dolphins

				W/L	TOTAL
*Keep track of wins and losses (**division games in bold**)*					
Week 1	Sun, Sep 10	4:25 PM	at Los Angeles Chargers	___	___/___
Week 2	Sun, Sep 17	8:20 PM	**at New England Patriots**	___	___/___
Week 3	Sun, Sep 24	1:00 PM	Denver Broncos	___	___/___
Week 4	Sun, Oct 1	1:00 PM	**at Buffalo Bills**	___	___/___
Week 5	Sun, Oct 8	1:00 PM	New York Giants	___	___/___
Week 6	Sun, Oct 15	1:00 PM	Carolina Panthers	___	___/___
Week 7	Sun, Oct 22	8:20 PM	at Philadelphia Eagles	___	___/___
Week 8	Sun, Oct 29	1:00 PM	**New England Patriots**	___	___/___
Week 9	Sun, Nov. 5	9:30 AM	Kansas City Chiefs*	___	___/___
Week 10	BYE WEEK				
Week 11	Sun, Nov 19	1:00 PM	Las Vegas Raiders	___	___/___
Week 12	Fri, Nov 24	3:00 PM	**at New York Jets**	___	___/___
Week 13	Sun, Dec 3	1:00 PM	at Washington Commanders	___	___/___
Week 14	Mon, Dec 11	8:15 PM	Tennessee Titans	___	___/___
Week 15	Sun, Dec 17	1:00 PM	**New York Jets**	___	___/___
Week 16	Sun, Dec 24	4:25 PM	Dallas Cowboys	___	___/___
Week 17	Sun, Dec 31	1:00 PM	at Baltimore Ravens	___	___/___
Week 18	Sun, Jan 7	TBD	**Buffalo Bills**	___	___/___

END OF SEASON RECORD:___/___

*international game

DIVISION TOTAL WIN/LOSS: ___/___

MINNESOTA VIKINGS

Head Coach: Kevin O'Connell | 2022 Record: 13-4
First Round Draft Pick: Jordan Addison, WR (23)

In typical fashion, Minnesota seems once again determined to snatch defeat from the jaws of victory. They have now released (not traded, just released) Dalvin Cook, the #6 running back in the league, without any clear plan for replacing him. We love Justin Jefferson as their #1 weapon on offense, but just like Buffalo or Chicago, can you succeed without a credible run game beyond your quarterback? Meanwhile, after finishing 31st in yards allowed and 28th in points allowed last year, the Vikings defense clearly needed an overhaul. Which they will get with new Defensive Coordinator Brian Flores. The NFC is wide open for wild card bidders, so Minnesota still has a decent shot to make the post-season, but we don't see them overcoming the 49ers or the Eagles to get to Las Vegas in February.

MINNESOTA VIKINGS

TEAM SCHEDULE
Minnesota Vikings

				W/L	TOTAL
ep track of wins and losses **(division games in bold)**					
Week 1	Sun, Sep 10	1:00 PM	Tampa Bay Buccaneers	___	___/___
Week 2	Thu, Sep 14	8:15 PM	at Philadelphia Eagles	___	___/___
Week 3	Sun, Sep 24	1:00 PM	Los Angeles Chargers	___	___/___
Week 4	Sun, Oct 1	1:00 PM	at Carolina Panthers	___	___/___
Week 5	Sun, Oct 8	4:25 PM	Kansas City Chiefs	___	___/___
Week 6	Sun, Oct 15	1:00 PM	**at Chicago Bears**	___	___/___
Week 7	Mon, Oct 23	8:15 PM	San Francisco 49ers	___	___/___
Week 8	Sun, Oct 29	1:00 PM	**at Green Bay Packers**	___	___/___
Week 9	Sun, Nov 5	1:00 PM	at Atlanta Falcons	___	___/___
Week 10	Sun, Nov 12	1:00 PM	New Orleans Saints	___	___/___
Week 11	Sun, Nov 19	8:20 PM	at Denver Broncos	___	___/___
Week 12	Mon, Nov 27	8:15 PM	**Chicago Bears**	___	___/___
Week 13	BYE WEEK				
Week 14	Sun, Dec 10	4:05 PM	at Las Vegas Raiders	___	___/___
Week 15	Sun, Dec 17	TBD	at Cincinnati Bengals	___	___/___
Week 16	Sun, Dec 24	1:00 PM	**Detroit Lions**	___	___/___
Week 17	Sun, Dec 31	8:20 PM	**Green Bay Packers**	___	___/___
Week 18	Sun, Jan 7	TBD	**at Detroit Lions**	___	___/___

END OF SEASON RECORD:___/___

DIVISION TOTAL WIN/LOSS: ___/___

NEW ENGLAND PATRIOTS

Head Coach: Bill Belichick | 2022 Record: 8-9
First Round Draft Pick: Christian Gonzalez, CB (17)

Who's on first? Wait, what game are we playing again? To say that the coaching staff for New England last year was clueless is as surprising as it is accurate. The greatest NFL coach in history muffs it? Yep. By refusing to hire a competent OC, by refusing to even designate a play caller, Belichik handcuffed his offense and wasted a year of his young QB's development. Enter Bill O'Brien. While we were no fans of O'Brien's GM performance in Houston, both he and Belichik seem to have figured out the right job for him in New England. Which should be very good news for Mac Jones. Meanwhile, the Patriots have had an outstanding defense for years, thanks to Belichik's prowess on that side of the ball. Put those together, and you've got... some massive competition in the AFC East, not to mention the rest of the Conference. After decades of riding a weak division to home field advantage in the playoffs, New England will be hard pressed to even make the playoffs this year. Times continue to be tough in the post-Brady era.

NEW ENGLAND PATRIOTS

New England Patriots

eep track of wins and losses (division games in bold)				W/L	TOTAL
Veek 1	Sun, Sep 10	4:25 PM	Philadelphia Eagles	___	___/___
Veek 2	Sun, Sep 17	8:20 PM	**Miami Dolphins**	___	___/___
Veek 3	Sun, Sep 24	1:00 PM	**at New York Jets**	___	___/___
Veek 4	Sun, Oct 1	4:25 PM	at Dallas Cowboys	___	___/___
Veek 5	Sun, Oct 8	1:00 PM	New Orleans Saints	___	___/___
Veek 6	Sun, Oct 15	4:05 PM	at Las Vegas Raiders	___	___/___
Veek 7	Sun, Oct 22	1:00 PM	**Buffalo Bills**	___	___/___
Veek 8	Sun, Oct 29	1:00 PM	**at Miami Dolphins**	___	___/___
Veek 9	Sun, Nov 5	1:00 PM	Washington Commanders	___	___/___
Veek 10	Sun, Nov 12	9:30 AM	Indianapolis Colts*	___	___/___
Veek 11	BYE WEEK				
Veek 12	Sun, Nov 26	1:00 PM	at New York Giants	___	___/___
Veek 13	Sun, Dec 3	1:00 PM	Los Angeles Chargers	___	___/___
Veek 14	Thu, Dec 7	8:15 PM	at Pittsburgh Steelers	___	___/___
Veek 15	Mon, Dec 18	8:15 PM	Kansas City Chiefs	___	___/___
Veek 16	Sun, Dec 24	8:15 PM	at Denver Broncos	___	___/___
Veek 17	Sun, Dec 31	1:00 PM	**at Buffalo Bills**	___	___/___
Veek 18	Sun, Jan 7	TBD	**New York Jets**	___	___/___

END OF SEASON RECORD:___/___

*nternational game

DIVISION TOTAL WIN/LOSS: ___/___

Head Coach: Dennis Allen | 2022 Record: 7-10
First Round Draft Pick: Bryan Bresee, DT (29)

Derek Carr gets a fresh start, and fans are hoping for a return to the days when starting QB wasn't even a question for the New Orleans Saints. This could actually be a really good fit. The Saints are in a very winnable division, and Carr should be happy with Michael Thomas, Chris Olave, Alvin Kamara, and Jamal Williams in the huddle. Meanwhile, the Saints boasted a top 10 defense last year in both yards per game and points per game. Add to that a gift from the scheduling gods — the second easiest schedule in the league, and we see the Saints back in the playoffs for 2023.

NEW ORLEANS SAINTS

TEAM SCHEDULE
New Orleans Saints

eep track of wins and losses (division games in bold)				W/L	TOTAL
Week 1	Sun, Sep 10	1:00 PM	Tennessee Titans	___	___/___
Week 2	Mon, Sep 18	7:15 PM	**at Carolina Panthers**	___	___/___
Week 3	Sun, Sep 24	1:00 PM	at Green Bay Packers	___	___/___
Week 4	Sun, Oct 1	1:00 PM	**Tampa Bay Buccaneers**	___	___/___
Week 5	Sun, Oct 8	1:00 PM	at New England Patriots	___	___/___
Week 6	Sun, Oct 15	1:00 PM	at Houston Texans	___	___/___
Week 7	Thu, Oct 19	8:15 PM	Jacksonville Jaguars	___	___/___
Week 8	Sun, Oct 29	1:00 PM	at Indianapolis Colts	___	___/___
Week 9	Sun, Nov 5	1:00 PM	Chicago Bears	___	___/___
Week 10	Sun, Nov 12	1:00 PM	at Minnesota Vikings	___	___/___
Week 11	BYE WEEK				
Week 12	Sun, Nov 26	1:00 PM	**at Atlanta Falcons**	___	___/___
Week 13	Sun, Dec 3	1:00 PM	Detroit Lions	___	___/___
Week 14	Sun, Dec 10	1:00 PM	**Carolina Panthers**	___	___/___
Week 15	Sun, Dec 17	1:00 PM	New York Giants	___	___/___
Week 16	Thu, Dec 21	8:15 PM	at Los Angeles Rams	___	___/___
Week 17	Sun, Dec 31	1:00 PM	**at Tampa Bay Buccaneers**	___	___/___
Week 18	Sun, Jan 7	TBD	**Atlanta Falcons**	___	___/___

END OF SEASON RECORD:___/___

DIVISION TOTAL WIN/LOSS: ___/___

NEW YORK GIANTS

Head Coach: Brian Daboll | 2022 Record: 9-7-1
First Round Pick: Deonte Banks, CB (24)

Daniel Jones got better, players around him got tougher, and Brian Daboll deserves a massive amount of credit for turning around a stalled franchise. But are we really convinced that the Giants can unseat the Eagles at the top of their division? Answer: no, we're not. Jones was better, largely because he cut down fumbles (way down), ran more (a lot more) and continued to throw well in the short game. But Jones only attempted 23 passes of 20 yards or more, so we have yet to see the kind of down-the-field power that drives post season success. And while Saquon Barkley had an exceptionally good year in 2022, counting on a repeat is betting against history. The defense last year was poor, though the team has made some nice moves to try to address that. The O-line, however, could be a real issue. Suffice it to say, we believe in Daboll, but there are just too many reasons to worry about the Giants.

NEW YORK GIANTS

TEAM SCHEDULE
New York Giants

				W/L	TOTAL
*...ep track of wins and losses (**division games in bold**)*					
Week 1	Sun, Sep 10	8:20 PM	**Dallas Cowboys**	___	___/___
Week 2	Sun, Sep 17	4:05 PM	at Arizona Cardinals	___	___/___
Week 3	Thu, Sep 21	8:15 PM	at San Francisco 49ers	___	___/___
Week 4	Mon, Oct 2	8:15 PM	Seattle Seahawks	___	___/___
Week 5	Sun, Oct 8	1:00 PM	at Miami Dolphins	___	___/___
Week 6	Sun, Oct 15	8:20 PM	at Buffalo Bills	___	___/___
Week 7	Sun, Oct 22	1:00 PM	**Washington Commanders**	___	___/___
Week 8	Sun, Oct 29	1:00 PM	New York Jets	___	___/___
Week 9	Sun, Nov 5	4:25 PM	at Las Vegas Raiders	___	___/___
Week 10	Sun, Nov 12	4:25 PM	**at Dallas Cowboys**	___	___/___
Week 11	Sun, Nov 19	1:00 PM	**at Washington Commanders**	___	___/___
Week 12	Sun, Nov 26	1:00 PM	New England Patriots	___	___/___
Week 13	BYE WEEK				
Week 14	Mon, Dec 11	8:15 PM	Green Bay Packers	___	___/___
Week 15	Sun, Dec 17	1:00 PM	at New Orleans Saints	___	___/___
Week 16	Mon, Dec 25	4:30 PM	**at Philadelphia Eagles**	___	___/___
Week 17	Sun, Dec 31	1:00 PM	Los Angeles Rams	___	___/___
Week 18	Sun, Jan 7	TBD	**Philadelphia Eagles**	___	___/___

END OF SEASON RECORD:___/___

DIVISION TOTAL WIN/LOSS: ___/___

NEW YORK JETS

Head Coach: Robert Saleh | 2022 Record: 7-10

First Round Pick: Will McDonald IV, Edge (15)

10 20 30 40 50 40 30 20 10

There hasn't been this much excitement in Jets fandom since Joe Namath donned a fur coat and promised New York a Super Bowl. Broadway Joe gave the Jets their only Super Bowl win in franchise history in 1969. Raise your hand if you were even alive then. In other words, it's been a really long wait. Enter Superstar #2: Aaron Rodgers. He looks confident, he looks comfortable, he looks happy. He was actually working out with his teammates before mandatory practices began. And that encompasses some very impressive, if young, talent — including both the offensive and defensive rookies of the year last year. Is New York's long Super Bowl drought finally over? Pump the brakes. Rodgers had a totally mediocre season last year, and he typically takes a while to warm up to new teammates, especially young ones. Perhaps his broken hand significantly hampered his play in 2022. Or maybe he's hit the age wall. Does he have one last run left? We can't wait to find out.

NEW YORK JETS

TEAM SCHEDULE
New York Jets

eep track of wins and losses (division games in bold)				W/L	TOTAL
Week 1	Mon, Sep 11	8:15 PM	**Buffalo Bills**	___	___/___
Week 2	Sun, Sep 17	4:25 PM	at Dallas Cowboys	___	___/___
Week 3	Sun, Sep 24	1:00 PM	**New England Patriots**	___	___/___
Week 4	Sun, Oct 1	8:20 PM	Kansas City Chiefs	___	___/___
Week 5	Sun, Oct 8	4:25 PM	at Denver Broncos	___	___/___
Week 6	Sun, Oct 15	4:25 PM	Philadelphia Eagles	___	___/___
Week 7	BYE WEEK				
Week 8	Sun, Oct 29	1:00 PM	at New York Giants	___	___/___
Week 9	Mon, Nov 6	8:15 PM	Los Angeles Chargers	___	___/___
Week 10	Sun, Nov 12	8:20 PM	at Las Vegas Raiders	___	___/___
Week 11	Sun, Nov 19	4:25 PM	**at Buffalo Bills**	___	___/___
Week 12	Fri, Nov 24	3:00 PM	**Miami Dolphins**	___	___/___
Week 13	Sun, Dec 3	1:00 PM	Atlanta Falcons	___	___/___
Week 14	Sun, Dec 10	1:00 PM	Houston Texans	___	___/___
Week 15	Sun, Dec 17	1:00 PM	**at Miami Dolphins**	___	___/___
Week 16	Sun, Dec 24	1:00 PM	Washington Commanders	___	___/___
Week 17	Thu, Dec 28	8:15 PM	at Cleveland Browns	___	___/___
Week 18	Sun, Jan 7	TBD	**at New England Patriots**	___	___/___

END OF SEASON RECORD:___/___

DIVISION TOTAL WIN/LOSS: ___/___

PHILADELPHIA EAGLES

Head Coach: Nick Siriani | 2022 Record: 14-3
First Round Draft Pick: Jalen Carter, DT (9); Nolan Smith, Edge (30)

Jalen gets better — I mean a lot better — he gets his team to the Super Bowl, and he gets paid. Great drama, happy ending. Will there be a sequel? We love the job Nick Siriani did with this team, and we have long been fans of GM Howie Roseman. Plus, the NFC is notoriously weak, with fewer and fewer elite QBs every time you turn around (wait, did we just call Jimmy G elite?). Like most Super Bowl teams, keeping everyone for another run is tough, but the Eagles kept many of their most important pieces. In addition to Hurts, they were able to retain their iconic center, Jason Kelce, as well as James Bradbury, Darius Slay, Fletcher Cox, Brandon Graham, Rashad Penny, and more. Add to that their offensive playmakers Davonta Smith, D'Andre Swift, Dallas Goedert, AJ Greene, plus two excellent Georgia Bulldogs in the first round, and Philadelphia still has pole position to win the NFC East, and play for another chance to represent the NFC in the Super Bowl.

PHILADELPHIA EAGLES

Philadelphia Eagles

eep track of wins and losses *(division games in bold)*				W/L	TOTAL
Week 1	Sun, Sep 10	4:25 PM	at New England Patriots	___	___/___
Week 2	Thu, Sep 14	8:15 PM	Minnesota Vikings	___	___/___
Week 3	Mon, Sep 25	7:15 PM	at Tampa Bay Buccaneers	___	___/___
Week 4	Sun, Oct 1	1:00 PM	**Washington Commanders**	___	___/___
Week 5	Sun, Oct 8	4:05 PM	at Los Angeles Rams	___	___/___
Week 6	Sun, Oct 15	4:25 PM	at New York Jets	___	___/___
Week 7	Sun, Oct 22	8:20 PM	Miami Dolphins	___	___/___
Week 8	Sun, Oct 29	1:00 PM	**at Washington Commanders**	___	___/___
Week 9	Sun, Nov 5	4:25 PM	**Dallas Cowboys**	___	___/___
Week 10	BYE WEEK				
Week 11	Mon, Nov 20	8:15 PM	at Kansas City Chiefs	___	___/___
Week 12	Sun, Nov 26	4:25 PM	Buffalo Bills	___	___/___
Week 13	Sun, Dec 3	4:25 PM	San Francisco 49ers	___	___/___
Week 14	Sun, Dec 10	8:20 PM	**at Dallas Cowboys**	___	___/___
Week 15	Sun, Dec 17	4:25 PM	at Seattle Seahawks	___	___/___
Week 16	Mon, Dec 25	4:30 PM	**New York Giants**	___	___/___
Week 17	Sun, Dec 31	1:00 PM	Arizona Cardinals	___	___/___
Week 18	Sun, Jan 7	TBD	**at New York Giants**	___	___/___

END OF SEASON RECORD:___/___

DIVISION TOTAL WIN/LOSS: ___/___

PITTSBURGH STEELERS

Head Coach: Mike Tomlin | 2022 Record: 9-8

First Round Draft Pick: Broderick Jones, OT (14)

Never doubt Mike Tomlin. I mean, just don't do it. Unlike some other head coaches we might name, Tomlin weathered the retirement of his franchise QB and still turned in a winning record with a rookie QB who entered the league without a lot of buzz and just got down to business. Whether or not Kenny Pickett will become the kind of dominant player that Big Ben was, is still a big question mark. But we like Pittsburgh's patient approach to developing their new young quarterback. On the defensive side, the Steelers remain reliably strong, boasting the top interception catcher in the league (Minkah Fitzpatrick) and ranking Top 10 in points allowed per game. If Pickett can take a step forward, Tomlin should continue his amazing streak of never-a-losing season.

PITTSBURGH STEELERS

Pittsburgh Steelers

				W/L	TOTAL
ep track of wins and losses **(division games in bold)**					
eek 1	Sun, Sep 10	1:00 PM	San Francisco 49ers	___	___/___
eek 2	Mon, Sep 18	8:15 PM	**Cleveland Browns**	___	___/___
eek 3	Sun, Sep 24	8:20 PM	at Las Vegas Raiders	___	___/___
eek 4	Sun, Oct 1	1:00 PM	at Houston Texans	___	___/___
eek 5	Sun, Oct 8	1:00 PM	**Baltimore Ravens**	___	___/___
eek 6	BYE WEEK				
eek 7	Sun, Oct 22	4:05 PM	at Los Angeles Rams	___	___/___
eek 8	Sun, Oct 29	1:00 PM	Jacksonville Jaguars	___	___/___
eek 9	Thu, Nov 2	8:15 PM	Tennessee Titans	___	___/___
eek 10	Sun, Nov 12	1:00 PM	Green Bay Packers	___	___/___
eek 11	Sun, Nov 19	1:00 PM	**at Cleveland Browns**	___	___/___
eek 12	Sun, Nov 26	1:00 PM	**at Cincinnati Bengals**	___	___/___
eek 13	Sun, Dec 3	1:00 PM	Arizona Cardinals	___	___/___
eek 14	Thu, Dec 7	8:15 PM	New England Patriots	___	___/___
eek 15	Sun, Dec 17	TBD	at Indianapolis Colts	___	___/___
eek 16	Sat, Dec 23	4:30 PM	**Cincinnati Bengals**	___	___/___
eek 17	Sun, Dec 31	4:05 PM	at Seattle Seahawks	___	___/___
eek 18	Sun, Jan 7	TBD	**at Baltimore Ravens**	___	___/___

END OF SEASON RECORD:___/___

DIVISION TOTAL WIN/LOSS: ___/___

SAN FRANCISCO 49'ERS

Head Coach: Kyle Shanahan | 2022 Record: 13-4
First Round Draft Pick: No Picks in Round 1

10
20
30
40
50
40
30
20
10

Repeat after me: I am relevant. I am relevant. I am relevant. Damn straight. How much fun was it to watch Mr. Irrelevant, the very last pick in the NFL draft, lead his team deep into the playoffs, and to fall short of the Super Bowl only by literally ripping the ligament of his throwing arm right off the bone? OK, that part wasn't fun — but the rest was pure Hollywood. Brock Purdy proved he is for real, not just a lucky beneficiary of Kyle Shanahan's quarterback-friendly system. And if his surgery and rehab go well, we love the 49ers' chances to get back to the NFC championship game, and this time to win it.

SAN FRANCISCO 49'ERS

TEAM SCHEDULE
San Francisco 49'ers

eep track of wins and losses *(division games in bold)*				W/L	TOTAL
Week 1	Sun, Sep 10	1:00 PM	at Pittsburgh Steelers	___	___/___
Week 2	Sun, Sep 17	4:05 PM	**at Los Angeles Rams**	___	___/___
Week 3	Thu, Sep 21	8:15 PM	New York Giants	___	___/___
Week 4	Sun, Oct 1	4:25 PM	**Arizona Cardinals**	___	___/___
Week 5	Sun, Oct 8	8:20 PM	Dallas Cowboys	___	___/___
Week 6	Sun, Oct 15	1:00 PM	at Cleveland Browns	___	___/___
Week 7	Mon, Oct 23	8:15 PM	at Minnesota Vikings	___	___/___
Week 8	Sun, Oct 29	4:25 PM	Cincinnati Bengals	___	___/___
Week 9	BYE WEEK				
Week 10	Sun, Nov 12	1:00 PM	at Jacksonville Jaguars	___	___/___
Week 11	Sun, Nov 19	4:05 PM	Tampa Bay Buccaneers	___	___/___
Week 12	Thu, Nov 23	8:20 PM	**at Seattle Seahawks**	___	___/___
Week 13	Sun, Dec 3	4:25 PM	at Philadelphia Eagles	___	___/___
Week 14	Sun, Dec 10	4:05 PM	**Seattle Seahawks**	___	___/___
Week 15	Sun, Dec 17	4:05 PM	**at Arizona Cardinals**	___	___/___
Week 16	Mon, Dec 25	8:15 PM	Baltimore Ravens	___	___/___
Week 17	Sun, Dec 31	1:00 PM	at Washington Commanders	___	___/___
Week 18	Sun, Jan 7	TBD	**Los Angeles Rams**	___	___/___

END OF SEASON RECORD: ___/___

DIVISION TOTAL WIN/LOSS: ___/___

SEATTLE SEAHAWKS

Head Coach: Pete Carroll | 2022 Record: 9-8

First Round Draft Pick: Devon Witherspoon, Edge (5); Jaxon Smith-Njigba, WR (20

No one likes "I told you so's" but it would be hard to blame Pete Carroll if he made that his IG handle. Trading Russell Wilson seemed like lunacy, and then sticking with Geno Smith as the starting QB? We're fine, he kept telling people. And then, they just kept winning. All the way to the playoffs, giving Geno Smith the pro-Bowl year he'd probably given up on ever having. So, let's not underestimate Pete again. Yes, he has to worry about San Francisco, but other than that, there isn't much standing in the way of the Seahawks going back to the playoffs in 2023. We're rooting for you, Geno.

SEATTLE SEAHAWKS

TEAM SCHEDULE
Seattle Seahawks

Keep track of wins and losses (division games in bold)				W/L	TOTAL
Week 1	Sun, Sep 10	4:25 PM	**Los Angeles Rams**	___	___/___
Week 2	Sun, Sep 17	1:00 PM	at Detroit Lions	___	___/___
Week 3	Sun, Sep 24	4:05 PM	Carolina Panthers	___	___/___
Week 4	Mon, Oct 2	8:15 PM	at New York Giants	___	___/___
Week 5	BYE WEEK				
Week 6	Sun, Oct 15	1:00 PM	at Cincinnati Bengals	___	___/___
Week 7	Sun, Oct 22	4:05 PM	**Arizona Cardinals**	___	___/___
Week 8	Sun, Oct 29	4:05 PM	Cleveland Browns	___	___/___
Week 9	Sun, Nov 5	1:00 PM	at Baltimore Ravens	___	___/___
Week 10	Sun, Nov 12	4:25 PM	Washington Commanders	___	___/___
Week 11	Sun, Nov 19	4:25 PM	**at Los Angeles Rams**	___	___/___
Week 12	Thu, Nov 23	8:20 PM	**San Francisco 49ers**	___	___/___
Week 13	Thu, Nov 30	8:15 PM	at Dallas Cowboys	___	___/___
Week 14	Sun, Dec 10	4:05 PM	**at San Francisco 49ers**	___	___/___
Week 15	Sun, Dec 17	4:25 PM	Philadelphia Eagles	___	___/___
Week 16	Sun, Dec 24	1:00 PM	at Tennessee Titans	___	___/___
Week 17	Sun, Dec 31	4:05 PM	Pittsburgh Steelers	___	___/___
Week 18	Sun, Jan 7	TBD	**at Arizona Cardinals**	___	___/___

END OF SEASON RECORD:___/___

DIVISION TOTAL WIN/LOSS: ___/___

TAMPA BAY BUCCANEERS

Head Coach: Todd Bowles | 2022 Record: 8-9
First Round Draft Pick: Calijah Kancey, DT (19)

It's finally over. Tom Brady has retired, and this time, it's for good. He looked great hitting that drone out of the sky with a perfect spiral, but we're pretty sure he'd rather throw a football off the stern of his $6-million yacht than on the grid iron. Who can blame him? We love you, Tom (said as a native New Englander), you deserve some me-time. Which leaves the Tampa Bay Buccaneers basically where it left the New England Patriots before them: stuck in mediocrity. We would love to predict that Baker Mayfield finally becomes the franchise quarterback many expected, but ... we'd also love to win the lottery. Ain't gonna happen.

TEAM SCHEDULE
Tampa Bay Buccaneers

ep track of wins and losses **(division games in bold)**				W/L	TOTAL
eek 1	Sun, Sep 10	1:00 PM	at Minnesota Vikings	___	___/___
eek 2	Sun, Sep 17	1:00 PM	Chicago Bears	___	___/___
eek 3	Mon, Sep 25	7:15 PM	Philadelphia Eagles	___	___/___
eek 4	Sun, Oct 1	1:00 PM	**at New Orleans Saints**	___	___/___
eek 5	BYE WEEK				
eek 6	Sun, Oct 15	1:00 PM	Detroit Lions	___	___/___
eek 7	Sun, Oct 22	1:00 PM	**Atlanta Falcons**	___	___/___
eek 8	Thu, Oct 26	8:15 PM	at Buffalo Bills	___	___/___
eek 9	Sun, Nov 5	1:00 PM	at Houston Texans	___	___/___
eek 10	Sun, Nov 12	1:00 PM	Tennessee Titans	___	___/___
eek 11	Sun, Nov 19	4:05 PM	at San Francisco 49ers	___	___/___
eek 12	Sun, Nov 26	1:00 PM	at Indianapolis Colts	___	___/___
eek 13	Sun, Dec 3	1:00 PM	**Carolina Panthers**	___	___/___
eek 14	Sun, Dec 10	1:00 PM	**at Atlanta Falcons**	___	___/___
eek 15	Sun, Dec 17	1:00 PM	at Green Bay Packers	___	___/___
eek 16	Sun, Dec 24	4:05 PM	Jacksonville Jaguars	___	___/___
eek 17	Sun, Dec 31	1:00 PM	**New Orleans Saints**	___	___/___
eek 18	Sun, Jan 7	TDB	**at Carolina Panthers**	___	___/___

END OF SEASON RECORD:___/___

DIVISION TOTAL WIN/LOSS: ___/___

TENNESSEE TITANS

Head Coach: Mike Vrabel | 2022 Record: 7-10
First Round Draft Pick: Peter Skoronski, OT (11)

All steak, no sizzle. That's the Vrabel recipe, built on strength and toughness, but lacking a star at QB. And now that Ryan Tannehill looks even less exciting than he did when Tennessee grabbed the #1 seed in the AFC a few years back, we're not quite sure it ever made sense to consider signing DeAndre Hopkins. Hopkins apparently felt the same way. So, what is the plan in Tennessee? The Titans have a consistently good defense, but when it comes to scoring points, Derrick Henry is incredible but another year older, and the receiving corps is underwhelming. Unless Vrabel has a surprise in store behind center (is that Will Levis warming up in the dugout?), we can't see how these pieces add up to a playoff run for the Titans.

TENNESSEE TITANS

TEAM SCHEDULE
Tennessee Titans

				W/L	TOTAL
eep track of wins and losses **(division games in bold)**					
Jeek 1	Sun, Sep 10	1:00 PM	at New Orleans Saints	___	___/___
Jeek 2	Sun, Sep 17	1:00 PM	Los Angeles Chargers	___	___/___
Jeek 3	Sun, Sep 24	1:00 PM	at Cleveland Browns	___	___/___
Jeek 4	Sun, Oct 1	1:00 PM	Cincinnati Bengals	___	___/___
Jeek 5	Sun, Oct 8	1:00 PM	**at Indianapolis Colts**	___	___/___
Jeek 6	Sun, Oct 15	9:30 AM	Baltimore Ravens*	___	___/___
Jeek 7	BYE WEEK				
Jeek 8	Sun, Oct 29	1:00 PM	Atlanta Falcons	___	___/___
Jeek 9	Thu, Nov 2	8:15 PM	at Pittsburgh Steelers	___	___/___
Jeek 10	Sun, Nov 12	1:00 PM	at Tampa Bay Buccaneers	___	___/___
Jeek 11	Sun, Nov 19	1:00 PM	**at Jacksonville Jaguars**	___	___/___
Jeek 12	Sun, Nov 26	1:00 PM	Carolina Panthers	___	___/___
Jeek 13	Sun, Dec 3	1:00 PM	**Indianapolis Colts**	___	___/___
Jeek 14	Mon, Dec 11	8:15 PM	at Miami Dolphins	___	___/___
Jeek 15	Sun, Dec 17	1:00 PM	**Houston Texans**	___	___/___
Jeek 16	Sun, Dec 24	1:00 PM	Seattle Seahawks	___	___/___
Jeek 17	Sun, Dec 31	1:00 PM	**at Houston Texans**	___	___/___
Jeek 18	Sun, Jan 7	TBD	**Jacksonville Jaguars**	___	___/___

END OF SEASON RECORD:___/___

international game

DIVISION TOTAL WIN/LOSS: ___/___

WASHINGTON COMMANDERS

Head Coach: Ron Rivera | 2022 Record: 8-8-1
First Round Draft Pick: Emmanuel Forbes, CB (16)

Riverboat Ron is probably getting ready to sail off into the sunset. Or get cut loose. New ownership is a healthy change, but they probably will not be patient. Without a convincing answer for quarterback, the Commanders look destined to come in last in the NFC East, and we just don't see enough offensive talent to change our minds. We are rooting for Eric Bieniemy to pull a rabbit out of this hat, but we're frustrated that he didn't get a head coaching job, and even more frustrated that he has to "prove" himself by making magic with Sam Howell. No offense, Sam.

WASHINGTON COMMANDERS

Washington Commanders

eep track of wins and losses **(division games in bold)**				W/L	TOTAL
Week 1	Sun, Sep 10	1:00 PM	Arizona Cardinals	___	___/___
Week 2	Sun, Sep 17	4:25 PM	at Denver Broncos	___	___/___
Week 3	Sun, Sep 24	1:00 PM	Buffalo Bills	___	___/___
Week 4	Sun, Oct 1	1:00 PM	**at Philadelphia Eagles**	___	___/___
Week 5	Thu, Oct 5	8:15 PM	Chicago Bears	___	___/___
Week 6	Sun, Oct 15	1:00 PM	at Atlanta Falcons	___	___/___
Week 7	Sun, Oct 22	1:00 PM	**at New York Giants**	___	___/___
Week 8	Sun, Oct 29	1:00 PM	**Philadelphia Eagles**	___	___/___
Week 9	Sun, Nov 5	1:00 PM	at New England Patriots	___	___/___
Week 10	Sun, Nov 12	4:25 PM	at Seattle Seahawks	___	___/___
Week 11	Sun, Nov 19	1:00 PM	**New York Giants**	___	___/___
Week 12	Thu, Nov 23	4:30 PM	**at Dallas Cowboys**	___	___/___
Week 13	Sun, Dec 3	1:00 PM	Miami Dolphins	___	___/___
Week 14	BYE WEEK				
Week 15	Sun, Dec 17	4:05 PM	at Los Angles Rams	___	___/___
Week 16	Sun, Dec 24	1:00 PM	at New York Jets	___	___/___
Week 17	Sun, Dec 31	1:00 PM	San Francisco 49ers	___	___/___
Week 18	Sun, Jan 7	TBD	**Dallas Cowboys**	___	___/___

END OF SEASON RECORD:___/___

DIVISION TOTAL WIN/LOSS: ___/___

Scorecard
Keep Track Of Your Weekly Results

How'd you do? Use this sheet to keep track of your own score each week.

	Wins	Losses	Your Net Score
Week 1	——	——	——
Week 2	——	——	——
Week 3	——	——	——
Week 4	——	——	——
Week 5	——	——	——
Week 6	——	——	——
Week 7	——	——	——
Week 8	——	——	——
Week 9	——	——	——
Week 10	——	——	——
Week 11	——	——	——
Week 12	——	——	——
Week 13	——	——	——
Week 14	——	——	——
Week 15	——	——	——
Week 16	——	——	——
Week 17	——	——	——
Week 18	——	——	——
TOTAL SCORE:		——	

Regular season finished? Time for the play-offs!

PLAYOFFS!

Final Standings at
End of 2022 Regular Season
(division winners in bold, wild card teams in italics)

NFC NORTH

Minnesota Vikings 13-4
Detroit Lions 9-8
Green Bay Packers 8-9
Chicago Bears 3-14

NFC SOUTH

Tampa Bay Buccaneers 8-9
New Orleans Saints 7-10
Atlanta Falcons 7-10
Carolina Panthers 7-10

NFC EAST

Philadelphia Eagles 14-3
Dallas Cowboys 12-5
New York Giants 9-7-1
Washington Commanders 8-8-1

NFC WEST

San Francisco 49ers 13-4
Seattle Seahawks 9-8
Los Angeles Rams 5-12
Arizona Cardinals 4-13

AFC NORTH

Cincinnati Bengals 12-4
Baltimore Ravens 10-7
Pittsburgh Steelers 9-8
Cleveland Browns 7-10

AFC SOUTH

Jacksonville Jaguars 9-8
Tennessee Titans 7-10
Indianapolis Colts 4-12-1
Houston Texans 3-13-1

AFC EAST

Buffalo Bills 13-3
Miami Dolphins 9-8
New England Patriots 8-9
New York Jets 7-10

AFC WEST

Kansas City Chiefs 14-3
Los Angeles Chargers 10-7
Las Vegas Raiders 6-11
Denver Broncos 5-12

Division Winners 2023

Fill in the division winners and wild cards, now that the regular season is done. Compare this to the predictions you made at the start of the season (back on page 5).

AFC

YOUR PREDICTIONS	ACTUAL WINNERS
North _____	North _____
South _____	South _____
East _____	East _____
West _____	West _____
Wild Card 1 _____	Wild Card 1 _____
Wild Card 2 _____	Wild Card 2 _____
Wild Card 3 _____	Wild Card 3 _____

NFC

YOUR PREDICTIONS	ACTUAL WINNERS
North _____	North _____
South _____	South _____
East _____	East _____
West _____	West _____
Wild Card 1 _____	Wild Card 1 _____
Wild Card 2 _____	Wild Card2 _____
Wild Card 3 _____	Wild Card 3 _____

How did you do?

Correct Total Number of Teams in Playoffs: _____

Correct Number of Division Winners: _____

Correct Number of Wild Card Winners: _____

2022 Playoff Results

(winners in bold/seeding in parentheses)

WILD CARD ROUND

NFC

(5) **Dallas Cowboys 31**	at	(4) Tampa Bay Buccaneers 14
(6) **New York Giants 31**	at	(3) Minnesota Vikings 24
(7) Seattle Seahawks 23	at	(2) **San Francisco 49ers 41**

AFC

(5) Los Angeles Chargers 30	at	(4) **Jacksonville Jaguars 31**
(6) Baltimore Ravens 17	at	(3) **Cincinnati Bengals 24**
(7) Miami Dolphins 31	at	(2) **Buffalo Bills 34**

DIVISIONAL ROUND

NFC

(5) Dallas Cowboys 12	at	(2) **San Francisco 49ers 19**
(6) New York Giants 7	at	(1) **Philadelphia Eagles 38**

AFC

(3) **Cincinnati Bengals 27**	at	(2) Buffalo Bills 10
(4) Jacksonville Jaguars 20	at	(1) **Kansas City Chiefs 27**

CONFERENCE CHAMPIONSHIPS

NFC

San Francisco 49ers 7	at	**Philadelphia Eagles 31**

AFC

Cincinnati Bengals 20	at	**Kansas City Chiefs 23**

SUPER BOWL 56

Philadelphia Eagles 35	vs.	**Kansas City Chiefs 38**

How the Playoff Match-Ups Work

Welcome to the playoffs! Now the best of the best match up for a chance to hoist the Lombardi Trophy. Remember: Seven teams per conference, including three wild card teams from each conference, will qualify for post-season play, for a total of 14 playoff teams.

Here's how it all comes together: In both the AFC and the NFC, there are four divisions. The team with the best record in each division goes to the playoffs, so there are your first eight playoff teams — four from the NFC, four from the AFC. Then the three teams from each conference with the best records *who didn't win their division* your six wild card teams. Wild card teams can come from any division in the conference, even the same division.

So, now you have your 14 teams, seven from the AFC, seven from the NFC. Four division champs and three wild cards from each conference. The four division champs are seeded #1–#4, based on their regular season records, the three wild card teams are seeded #5, #6, and #7, again based on their records.

Only the #1 seed in each conference gets a bye. All six other playoff teams from each conference must play in wild-card weekend. Those teams are matched up as follows: the #2 seed in each conference plays the #7 seed in that conference; the #3 seeds play the #6 seeds; and the #4 seeds plays the #5 seeds.

The second week of the playoffs (the divisional round) you have eight teams left — the six that won their games in wild-card weekend, and the two teams that got a bye in the previous week. Here's how those eight teams play: in each conference, the #1 seed (well rested after their week off) plays the lowest seeded team still alive; while the remaining two teams in the conference play each other.

By week three (conference championship round), you just have four teams left — the winners of the previous weekend's four games. The two remaining AFC teams face off; the two remaining NFC teams face off, all now vying to be AFC or NFC conference champions.

And finally, the AFC champs meet the NFC champs for Super Bowl VIII, hosted for the first time ever in Las Vegas, on February 11, 2024.

On Page 94, you can see how the match-ups worked last year. What will the road to the Super Bowl look like this season? Turn to page 96 and take your best shot at predicting what will happen in this year's playoffs!

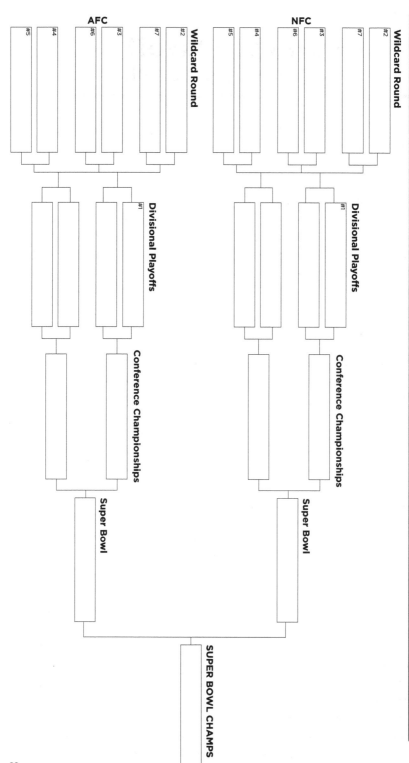

2023 Playoff Bracket Predictions
Fill In Your Picks at the Start of the Playoffs

NFC

Wildcard Round

#2
#7
#3
#6
#4
#5

Divisional Playoffs

#1

Conference Championships

Super Bowl

AFC

Wildcard Round

#2
#7
#3
#6
#4
#5

Divisional Playoffs

#1

Conference Championships

Super Bowl

SUPER BOWL CHAMPS

2023 Playoff Bracket Tracker
Keep Track of Playoff Results in Real Time

SUPER BOWL CHAMPS

#1

#1

#2

#7

#3

#6

#4

#5

#2

#7

#3

#6

#4

#5

SUPER BOWL WINNERS (AND LOSERS) FROM 1967-2023

Super Bowl Winners and Losers

1967–2023

Year	Winner		Loser	
1967	Green Bay Packers	35	Kansas City Chiefs	10
1968	Green Bay Packers	33	Oakland Raiders	14
1969	New York Jets	16	Baltimore Colts	7
1970	Kansas City Chiefs	23	Minnesota Vikings	7
1971	Baltimore Colts	16	Dallas Cowboys	13
1972	Dallas Cowboys	24	Miami Dolphins	3
1973	Miami Dolphins	14	Washington Redskins	7
1974	Miami Dolphins	24	Minnesota Vikings	7
1975	Pittsburgh Steelers	16	Minnesota Vikings	6
1976	Pittsburgh Steelers	21	Dallas Cowboys	17
1977	Oakland Raiders	32	Minnesota Vikings	14
1978	Dallas Cowboys	27	Denver Broncos	10
1979	Pittsburgh Steelers	35	Dallas Cowboys	31
1980	Pittsburgh Steelers	31	Los Angeles Rams	19
1981	Oakland Raiders	27	Philadelphia Eagles	10
1982	San Francisco 49ers	26	Cincinnati Bengals	21
1983	Washington Redskins	27	Miami Dolphins	17
1984	Los Angeles Raiders	38	Washington Redskins	9
1985	San Francisco 49ers	38	Miami Dolphins	16
1986	Chicago Bears	46	New England Patriots	10
1987	New York Giants	39	Denver Broncos	20
1988	Washington Redskins	42	Denver Broncos	10

Year	Winner		Loser	
1989	San Francisco 49ers	20	Cincinnati Bengals	16
1990	San Francisco 49ers	55	Denver Broncos	10
1991	New York Giants	20	Buffalo Bills	19
1992	Washington Redskins	37	Buffalo Bills	24
1993	Dallas Cowboys	52	Buffalo Bills	17
1994	Dallas Cowboys	30	Buffalo Bills	13
1995	San Francisco 49ers	49	San Diego Chargers	26
1996	Dallas Cowboys	27	Pittsburgh Steelers	17
1997	Green Bay Packers	35	New England Patriots	21
1998	Denver Broncos	31	Green Bay Packers	24
1999	Denver Broncos	34	Atlanta Falcons	19
2000	St. Louis Rams	23	Tennessee Titans	16
2001	Baltimore Ravens	34	New York Giants	7
2002	New England Patriots	20	St. Louis Rams	17
2003	Tampa Bay Buccaneers	48	Oakland Raiders	21
2004	New England Patriots	32	Carolina Panthers	29
2005	New England Patriots	24	Philadelphia Eagles	29
2006	Pittsburgh Steelers	21	Seattle Seahawks	10
2007	Indianapolis Colts	29	Chicago Bears	17
2008	New York Giants	17	New England Patriots	14
2009	Pittsburgh Steelers	27	Arizona Cardinals	23
2010	New Orleans Saints	31	Indianapolis Colts	17
2011	Green Bay Packers	31	Pittsburgh Steelers	25
2012	New York Giants	21	New England Patriots	17
2013	Baltimore Ravens	34	San Francisco 49ers	31
2014	Seattle Seahawks	43	Denver Broncos	8

Year	Winner		Loser	
2015	New England Patriots	28	Seattle Seahawks	2
2016	Denver Broncos	24	Carolina Panthers	1(
2017	New England Patriots	34	Atlanta Falcons	2
2018	Philadelphia Eagles	41	New England Patriots	3
2019	New England Patriots	13	Los Angeles Rams	3
2020	Kansas City Chiefs	31	San Francisco 49ers	2
2021	Tampa Bay Buccaneers	31	Kansas City Chiefs	9
2022	Los Angeles Rams	23	Cincinnati Bengals	2
2023	Kansas City Chiefs	38	Philadelphia Eagle	3

Reserve Your Copy of the 2024 Edition of *Are You Ready for Some Football* now!

s the dog days of summer drag on and you pretend to care about aseball, wouldn't it be fun to start getting ready for the 2024 football eason? Review your team's match-ups for the upcoming season, check ut who's on tap for Thursday nights, Sunday nights, Monday nights, fill ut your playoff predictions, and get ready for some football!

All you need to do is send me an email now at **MGRoss.Football@gmail.com**. ust let me know you might be interested in getting a copy of next year's uide. There's no commitment at all — except on my part: I will let you know s soon as the League releases its 2024 game schedules, and I will also let ou know when the 2024 guide will be ready for purchase.

It's an easy way to make sure you don't miss a thing. Because, if you 'e anything like me, you are ALWAYS ready for some football!

M.G.Ross
MGRoss.Football@gmail.com

Made in United States
Troutdale, OR
09/11/2023

12803736R00066